YOUR KNOWLEDGE HAS VALUE

- We will publish your bachelor's and master's thesis, essays and papers

- Your own eBook and book - sold worldwide in all relevant shops

- Earn money with each sale

Upload your text at www.GRIN.com and publish for free

Kristin Piepenburg

Critical analysis of Hofstede's model of cultural dimensions

To what extent are his findings reliable, valid and applicable to organisations in the 21st century?

GRIN Publishing

Bibliographic information published by the German National Library:

The German National Library lists this publication in the National Bibliography; detailed bibliographic data are available on the Internet at http://dnb.dnb.de .

This book is copyright material and must not be copied, reproduced, transferred, distributed, leased, licensed or publicly performed or used in any way except as specifically permitted in writing by the publishers, as allowed under the terms and conditions under which it was purchased or as strictly permitted by applicable copyright law. Any unauthorized distribution or use of this text may be a direct infringement of the author s and publisher s rights and those responsible may be liable in law accordingly.

Imprint:

Copyright © 2011 GRIN Verlag GmbH
Print and binding: Books on Demand GmbH, Norderstedt Germany
ISBN: 978-3-640-88157-4

This book at GRIN:

http://www.grin.com/en/e-book/169716/critical-analysis-of-hofstede-s-model-of-cultural-dimensions

GRIN - Your knowledge has value

Since its foundation in 1998, GRIN has specialized in publishing academic texts by students, college teachers and other academics as e-book and printed book. The website www.grin.com is an ideal platform for presenting term papers, final papers, scientific essays, dissertations and specialist books.

Visit us on the internet:

http://www.grin.com/

http://www.facebook.com/grincom

http://www.twitter.com/grin_com

CRITICAL ANALYSIS OF HOFSTEDE'S MODEL OF CULTURAL DIMENSIONS:

TO WHAT EXTENT ARE HIS FINDINGS RELIABLE, VALID AND APPLICABLE TO ORGANISATIONS IN THE 21ST CENTURY?

Kristin Piepenburg

Dissertation submitted to Oxford Brookes University for the partial fulfilment of the requirement for the degree of MASTER OF SCIENCE in BUSINESS MANAGEMENT

(January 2011)

ABSTRACT

Critical analysis of Hofstede's model of cultural dimensions: To what extent are his findings reliable, valid and applicable to organisations in the 21st century?

Kristin Piepenburg

28th January 2011

Global markets are changing faster than ever and increasing international competition makes it necessary for managers to understand not only the domestic culture but also the host country's culture.

Derived from globalisation, successful cross-cultural management is gaining in importance and its need for understanding of cultural differences becomes essential. Because of this it is argued that, with the increasing importance of a cross-cultural understanding, Hofstede's (1980) model of cultural dimensions gains proportional importance and attracts notice at the same time. His study is widely used in global operating organisations within trainings and workshops. The first step of effective cross-cultural management is the awareness that cultural differences exist and domestic strategies might fail in host countries

Even though, Hofstede's (1980) cultural study is the most important one and widely knows, there are many other cultural studies, which are only partly supporting his study. For each and every model of cultural identifications arouse praise and criticism and Hofstede was not spared by criticism. The main criticism refers to the methodology Hofstede used and many authors questioned its validity and reliability. Another major critique is that the nearly 40-years old survey findings are out-dated and not of any modern value anymore. Addressing the elaborated criticisms from the literature, a personal replication study within the two countries of Germany and the UK is undertaken in order to evaluate the validity, reliability and applicability in the 21st century. This study has developed own dimension scores for Masculinity/ Femininity (MAS) and Uncertainty Avoidance (UA) for Germany and the UK and compared and evaluated these with Hofstede's findings. The findings of this study vary from Hofstede's findings, as according to this study the UK is more masculine and has a higher Uncertainty Avoidance score than Germany. These findings do not support Hofstede's findings and further cultural research is recommended.

CONTENTS

chapter	page

ABSTRACT ii

LIST OF TABLES vi

LIST OF FIGURES viii

LIST OF ABBREVIATIONS x

CHAPTER 1 1

1 INTRODUCTION 1

1.1   GLOBALISATION 2

1.2   CROSS-CULTURAL MANAGEMENT 3

1.3   NEED FOR CONTEMPORARY APPROACH 4

1.4   RESEARCH AIM AND OBJECTIVES 5

    1.4.1   Aim 5

    1.4.2   Objectives 6

1.5   OUTLINE OF THE CHAPTERS 7

CHAPTER 2 8

2 LITERATURE REVIEW 8

2.1   CULTURE DEFINED 8

    2.1.1   National culture 12

    2.1.2   Organisational culture 13

2.2   HOFSTEDE'S STUDY OF CULTURAL DIMENSIONS 14

    2.2.1   Research data 15

    2.2.2   Cultural dimensions 16

    2.2.3   Other cultural studies and comparison with Hofstede's dimensions 22

2.3   ANALYSIS AND EVALUATION OF HOFSTEDE'S FINDINGS 30

    2.3.1   Arguments in support of Hofstede's study 31

    2.3.2   Arguments against Hofstede's study 33

    2.3.3   Discussion 40

2.4   HOFSTEDE'S FINDINGS IN PRACTICE 41

CHAPTER 3 44

3 RESEARCH METHODOLOGY 44

3.1	RESEARCH PROCESS		44
	3.1.1	Philosophy of research	45
	3.1.2	Research Approach	46
	3.1.3	Research Strategy	48
	3.1.4	Research Choices	49
	3.1.5	Time Horizon	49
	3.1.6	Data collection method	50
3.2	DATA VALIDITY, RELIABILITY AND GENERALISIBILITY		59
	3.2.1	Validity	59
	3.2.2	Reliability	61
	3.2.3	Generalisability	63
3.3	RESEARCH ETHICS		63
3.4	LIMITATIONS		64

CHAPTER 4		**66**
4	**ANALYSIS AND FINDINGS**	**66**
4.1	INTRODUCTION	66
4.2	CALCULATION OF DIMENSION SCORES	67
4.3	MASCULINITY	70
	4.3.1 MAS Index Score	70
	4.3.2 Further Analysis	75
4.4	UNCERTAINTY AVOIDANCE	78
	4.4.1 UA Index Score	78
	4.4.2 Further Analysis	86
4.5	DISCUSSION	88

CHAPTER 5		**91**
5	**CONCLUSION AND RECOMMENDATIONS**	**91**
5.1	CONCLUSION	91
5.2	FUTURE RESEARCH AND RECOMMENDATION	94

REFERENCES	**95**
APPENDICES	**107**

LIST OF TABLES

table	page

TABLE I: TROMPENAARS 7 DIMENSIONS 24

TABLE II: SCHWARTZ'S DIMENSIONS 25

TABLE III: KLUCKHOHN'S AND STRODTBECK'S DIMENSION 25

TABLE IV: HALL AND HALL COMMUNICATION STYLES 26

TABLE V: HALL AND HALL TIME ORIENTATION 26

TABLE VI: GLOBE DIMENSIONS 27

TABLE VII: COMPARISON OF CULTURAL STUDIES 29

TABLE VIII: ARGUMENTS FOR AND AGAINST HOFSTEDE'S STUDY 30

TABLE IX: EXAMPLES OF PRACTICAL APPLICATIONS OF HOFSTEDE'S WORK 42

TABLE X: KEY ELEMENTS OF EMPLOYEES IN INDIVIDUALISTIC CULTURES 43

TABLE XI: ADVANTAGES AND DISADVANTAGES OF QUESTIONNAIRES 48

TABLE XII: ADVANTAGES AND DISADVANTAGES OF SECONDARY DATA 51

TABLE XIII: ADVANTAGES AND DISADVANTAGES OF PRIMARY DATA 52

TABLE XIV: MAIN ATTRIBUTES OF SELF-ADMINISTERED DELIVERY AND COLLECTION QUESTIONNAIRES 56

TABLE XV: THIS STUDY MAS EQUATION 70

TABLE XVI: THIS STUDY'S MAS COMPARED WITH HOFSTEDE'S MAS .. 71

TABLE XVII: CALCULATED GENDER MAS 76

TABLE XVIII: THIS STUDY UA EQUATION 79

TABLE XIX: THIS STUDY'S UA COMPARED WITH HOFSTEDE'S UA 79

TABLE XX: THIS STUDY'S MAS COMPARED TO HOFSTEDE'S MAS........89

TABLE XXI: THIS STUDY'S UA COMAPRED TO HOFSTEDE'S UA............89

TABLE XXII: ARGUMENTS FOR AND AGAINST HOFSTEDE'S STUDY 92

TABLE XXIII: THIS STUDY'S FINDINGS..92

LIST OF FIGURES

figure   page

FIGURE 1: THE 'ICEBERG' MODEL OF CULTURE...9

FIGURE 2: THE 'ONION DIAGRAM': MANIFESTATIONS OF CULTURE AT DIFFERENT LEVELS OF DEPTH...11

FIGURE 3: COMPARISON OF HOFSTEDE'S CULTURAL DIMENSION WITH OTHER CULTURAL STUDIES...23

FIGURE 4: THE RESEARCH ONION...44

FIGURE 5: PROCESS OF DEDUCTION...46

FIGURE 6: SAMPLE AGE AVERAGE...53

FIGURE 7: SURVEY SAMPLE...54

FIGURE 8: TYPES OF QUESTIONNAIRES...55

FIGURE 9: STAGES THAT MUST OCCUR IF A QUESTION IS TO BE VALID AND RELIABLE...59

FIGURE 10: QUESTION 10F) COOPERATION...72

FIGURE 11: QUESTION 10B) RECOGNITION...72

FIGURE 12: QUESTION 10G) LIVING AREA...73

FIGURE 13: QUESTION 10C) ADVANCEMENT...73

FIGURE 14: AVERAGES OF INDICATOR QUESTIONS...74

FIGURE 15: AVERAGES OF MASCULINITY ATTRIBUTED QUESTIONS...75

FIGURE 16: AVERAGES OF FEMININITY ATTRIBUTED QUESTIONS.......75

FIGURE 17: GENDER DISTRIBUTION...75

FIGURE 18: QUESTION 9 GERMANY...77

FIGURE 19: QUESTION 9 UK...77

FIGURE 20: QUESTION 2...80

FIGURE 21: QUESTION 1...81

FIGURE 22: QUESTION 5...81

FIGURE 23: QUESTION 3 82

FIGURE 24: UA INDICATOR QUESTIONS 83

FIGURE 25: UA QUESTIONS 84

FIGURE 26: HIGH AND LOW UA QUESTIONS 85

FIGURE 27: QUESTION 4 AND 6 86

FIGURE 28: QUESTION 8 87

FIGURE 29: JOB SECURITY 88

LIST OF ABBREVIATIONS

C	Constant
CVS	Chinese Value Survey
EVS	European Value Survey
GLOBE	Global Leadership and Organizational Behaviour Effectiveness
GNP	Gross National Product
HF	Hochschule Fresenius (University of Applied Science, Fresenius), Cologne Germany
IBM	International Business Machines
ID	Individualism
IDV	Individualism/ Collectivism dimension
IVR	Indulgence vs. Restraint dimension
LTO	Long-term Orientation dimension
OBU	Oxford Brookes University
MAS	Masculinity/ Femininity dimension
MNC	Multinational Company
UA	Uncertainty Avoidance
UAI	Uncertainty Avoidance Index
UK	United Kingdom
PD	Power Distance
PDI	Power Distance Index
VSM	Value Survey Module
WVS	World Value Survey

CHAPTER 1

1 INTRODUCTION

'We may have all come on different ships, but we're in the same boat now'.

Martin Luther King Jr.

Martin Luther King Junior's quotation encapsulates the issue cross-cultural management is dealing with. The 'same' boat stands metaphorically for cross-border relations and international businesses, and the 'different' ships for the employees and managers of an organisation who come from different countries, cultures and backgrounds. To be able to manoeuvre the boat in the right direction, the captain and the crew have to pull together. The same applies to international and cross-border businesses and to be able to work together effectively the need for understanding of each other's background is essential. It is argued that, only if you know where all the ships and its members come from, you will know how to get the best out of this crew and be able to reach the final destination. Therefore, to protect cross-cultural activities from failing and use them effectively, Hofstede (1980) developed cultural dimensions to identify cultural differences and to help and support the ship to reach its final destination.

Global markets are changing faster than ever and 'in today's increasingly competitive and demanding international free market economy, managers cannot succeed on their understanding of domestic culture alone' (Parhizgar, 2002, p. 2). Derived from globalisation, successful cross-cultural management is gaining in importance and the need for an understanding of cultural differences becomes necessary. It is argued that, simultaneously with the increasing importance of a cross-cultural understanding, Hofstede's (1980) model of cultural dimensions gains proportional importance and attracts notice at the same time (Peterson, 2007).

1.1 GLOBALISATION

'Globalization can be defined as the process by which markets and production in different countries are becoming increasingly interdependent due to dynamics of trade in goods and services and flows of capital and technology' (Held, 2000, p.92). Furthermore, Leidner (2010, p.69) states that globalisation 'also encompass the exchange of production materials, the substitution of production processes, the relocation of services, the redistribution of resources, and the diffusion and infusion of cultural norms, artifacts, and values'.

According to Bourguignon *et al.* (2002), globalisation is a centuries-old phenomenon and Scholte (2000) concludes that interconnections and trades between countries took place before the word 'globalisation' actually was established. But 'there is still a great deal of uncertainty surrounding its meaning and use of international business' (Fletcher, 2000, p.211) and some authors, like Rugman (2003, p.409) even have the opinion that 'globalisation is a myth' and does not exist. He believes that the trend towards globalisation does not exist and that most business activities of large international firms do not take place in one single global market but within regional blocks. Moreover, Rugman (2005) states that managers need to design regional strategies rather than global ones. Stevens and Bird (2004, p.509) question Rugman and offer a detailed critique leading to the conclusion that 'globalization is very much alive and well'.

Moreover, Hofstede *et al.* (2010) deepens the discussion of vanishing boundaries by implementing the notion of the 'global village', which makes the world appear smaller due to the World Wide Web and fast developing technologies.

Globalisation is affecting businesses and life all over the world. Alongside with its strengths and advantages, there are also weaknesses and disadvantages. The global weakness has just taken place in form of the global financial crisis, which has shaken markets worldwide and led Iceland into bankruptcy (Amadeo, 2008; Cline, 2010). Furthermore, Hofstede (2009a) blames the USA, where the financial crisis started and the interdependence of the modern global economy for the huge impact of the crisis and the long lasting consequences. His study and observation of MBA students from 17 countries analysed the objective of their country's business leaders (Hofstede *et al.*, 2002). Resulting from this study he characterised US business leaders as 'greedy, short-term gain oriented, and out of power' (Hofstede, 2009a, p. 309) and concludes that this short-term orientation and greediness of the Americans are the main drivers of the financial crisis. Hofstede (2009a) states further, that the crisis could have been predicted, even though he adds that he did not have the necessary perspicacity for a perfect solution.

Business companies operate worldwide and 'mergers, acquisitions, joint ventures, and alliances across national borders have become frequent, but they remain a regular source of cross-cultural clashes' (Hofstede *et al.*, 2010, p.407). Therefore cross-cultural management and multiculturalism has become an essential topic for Multinational Companies (MNC) (Parhizgar, 2002, p. xiii).

1.2 CROSS-CULTURAL MANAGEMENT

'In the light of globalization and the rapid changes facing the world the need for understanding how people from different cultures interact and communicate has assumed a staggering importance' (Bhawuk, 2008, p. 305). The awareness of cultural differences is becoming more essential in nowadays global businesses and is affecting cross-cultural management.

Therefore it is important for MNCs and their managers to develop cultural awareness to sustain management effectiveness across cultural borders (Trompenaar and Hampden-Turner, 1997). Furthermore managers need multicultural interactive skills to be able to understand the differences of domestic culture and the culture of the country they would like to operate in (Parhizgar, 2002). To prepare managers and expatriates and help them to understand the impact of cultural differences as well as how they can deal with it, appropriate training and teaching is needed (Swierczek, 1994).

The growing interest of the on-going debate about cross-cultural differences and its influence on managerial behaviour was initiated by Hofstede (1980) who developed a model which identified several dimensions of cultural differences (Warner and Joynt, 2002). This model has been used ever since for explaining cultural differences and to investigate adequate manager's behaviour in other countries. However, the question is to what extent Hofstede's (1980) model is really helping managers to understand these cultural differences and how managers can benefit from his model in everyday life.

1.3 NEED FOR CONTEMPORARY APPROACH

'Undoubtedly, the most significant cross-cultural study of work-related values is the one carried out by Hofstede' (Bhagat and McQuaid, 1982, cited in Jones, 2007, p.2). Hofstede's (1980) book 'Culture's Consequences' was published at a time where little research about culture had been done, especially related to cross-cultural relationships of organisations. The interest in cultural differences was rising due to organisations entering global markets and expanding worldwide (Hofstede *et al.*, 2010). Hofstede (1980) and his identified cultural dimensions, which are explained more detailed in Chapter 2.2., shaped a foundation and guideline for understanding culture and created a driving force for other researchers to continue (Powell, 2006). Researchers have described his study as the most important paradigm 'for the study of culture and business management' (Dawson and Young, 2003, p.587) and the cause of enormous numbers of citations, replications and discussions (Fang, 2003).

However, his study and findings are broadly discussed and criticised and many scholars have attempted to complement, update and even challenged his original study (Gooderham and Nordhaug, 2001). Moreover, the main critique is the out-dated and old-fashioned character of Hofstede's (1980) study. Therefore, it is argued that there is a need to complement Hofstede's (1980) study with a contemporary approach. Even though, Hofstede (1980; 2001) claims that culture stays stable over time and merely changes slowly, many researchers disagree and state that culture shifts over time. This study seeks to find out to what extent Hofstede's (1980) study is still relevant in the 21st century and analyses its validity and reliability nowadays.

1.4 RESEARCH AIM AND OBJECTIVES

In the following section the research aim and objectives are introduced.

1.4.1 Aim

The aim and purpose of this study is to analyse and evaluate Hofstede's (1980) study of cultural dimensions and its reliability, its validity and to what extent it is applicable to organisations in the 21st century.

This study aims to meet the need for a contemporary approach of Hofstede's (1980) findings and contribute to the discussion of cultural studies by analysing contemporary cultural differences between Germany and the United Kingdom (UK) and in how far they vary from Hofstede's (1980; 2001) findings. Moreover, the critiques of Hofstede's study and methodology are considered and an own indicating replication study of the cultural dimensions of Masculinity/ Femininity (MAS) and Uncertainty Avoidance (UA) is undertaken.

A practical context is made within the analysis to figure out to what extent an application of Hofstede's (1980) study in organisations is helping managers in everyday life regarding cross-cultural management and activities.

1.4.2 Objectives

1. To analyse Hofstede's (1980) study of cultural dimensions and identify as well as evaluate critique for and against his study

2. To identify similarities and differences of Hofstede's (1980) study with other cultural studies

3. To investigate the practical use and applicability of his study and to what extent managers benefit from it in cross-cultural management

4. To analyse and investigate the present differences of German and British students regarding the cultural dimensions of Masculinity and Uncertainty Avoidance and evaluate the following Hypotheses:

    H_1: The cultural dimension of Masculinity/ Femininity has not changed over time and Germany and UK are still very masculine countries with similar scores (66).

    H_2: The cultural dimension of Uncertainty Avoidance has not changed over time and Germany still scores higher (65) than the UK (35).

5. To compare the findings of the primary research with Hofstede's (1980) findings and analyse the differences

6. To be able to recommend improvements for cultural studies and future research.

1.5 OUTLINE OF THE CHAPTERS

This study comprises five chapters, which are outlined subsequently.

The first chapter presents the introductory section of the research topic and identifies the aim and the objectives of this study.

The second chapter reviews the main literature concerning culture, cultural differences, and cultural studies. It further explains, criticises, evaluates and compares Hofstede's (1980) study with other cultural studies. An investigation of the practical use and the applicability of Hofstede's (1980) study is provided and gives an insight in the value Hofstede adds to cross-cultural management.

In the third chapter the research methodology is specified and highlights philosophies, approaches and strategies that are used within this study. Moreover, the advantages, disadvantages and limitations of the applied research methods are assessed.

The Analysis and Findings, derived from the primary research are presented in the fourth chapter and present the main body of this study. The findings are analysed and compared to the findings from the literature review to gain a deeper understanding of the differences and similarities with Hofstede's (1980) study.

In the final chapter five, a summary of the findings for the previous chapters and a conclusion is given. This dissertation ends up in recommendations for future research in the field of cross-cultural management and cultural studies.

CHAPTER 2

2 LITERATURE REVIEW

This Chapter explains, defines and analyses the main elements of this study and gives an insight into the existing literature about culture, cultural differences and the variety of cultural studies. Hofstede's (1980) study is introduced, explained, criticised, evaluated and compared with other cultural studies. Moreover, Hofstede's (1980) findings and its practical use are discussed. The literature review is the basis for the Research Methodology and the Analysis and frames the Research Process.

2.1 CULTURE DEFINED

The word 'culture' has its origins in the Latin word *cultura*, which is related to *cultus*. This means cult or worship. In Latin, *cult* means to inhabit, till or worship and *are* means the result of. Thus, culture can be said to mean: *the result of human action* (Warner & Joynt, 2002).

Even though numerous researchers have dealt with the topic of culture, it could not have been agreed about a general definition so far. When Kroeber and Kluckhohn (1952) wrote their review on culture, they found 164 definitions of culture by anthropologists. Kluckhohn (1951, p.86) defines culture for examples as:

> 'Culture consists of patterned ways of thinking, feeling and reacting, acquired and transmitted mainly by symbols, constituting the distinctive achievements of human groups, including their embodiments in artifacts; the essential core of culture consist of traditional ideas and especially their attached values.'

Similarly, Peterson (2004, p.17) defines culture as 'the relatively stable set of inner values and beliefs generally held by groups of people in countries or regions and the noticeable impact those values and beliefs have on the peoples' outward behaviours and environment'.

However, the most cited definition is the one provided by Hofstede (1980, p.26): 'culture is the collective programming of the mind that distinguishes the members of one human group from another'.

Comparing all different definitions and taking them together, Hodgetts and Luthans (2003) identified six characteristics of culture. First, culture is learned, not inherited. Second, it is shared. Culture is not specific to a single individual, but it is shared by groups, organisations-, or entire societies. Third, culture is passed on from generation to generation. Fourth, culture is symbolic. Something can have entirely diverse meanings in different cultures, as it defines how the world is perceived and how life is organised. Fifth, culture is patterned. This means that it is integrated; if one aspect of culture changes, other parts are affected as well. Finally, culture is adaptive (Hoecklin, 1995; Hofstede, 1997; Trompenaars & Hampden-Turner, 1997). As the previous point already suggests, culture is dynamic. It is based on humans, who are able to change and adapt. But due to the difficulty of changing the minds of a whole nation, this occurs to be a very slow process (Hodgetts & Luthans, 2003).

Besides, it is agreed by most researchers that culture has visible and invisible elements, which can be illustrated as an iceberg as it is shown in Figure 2.

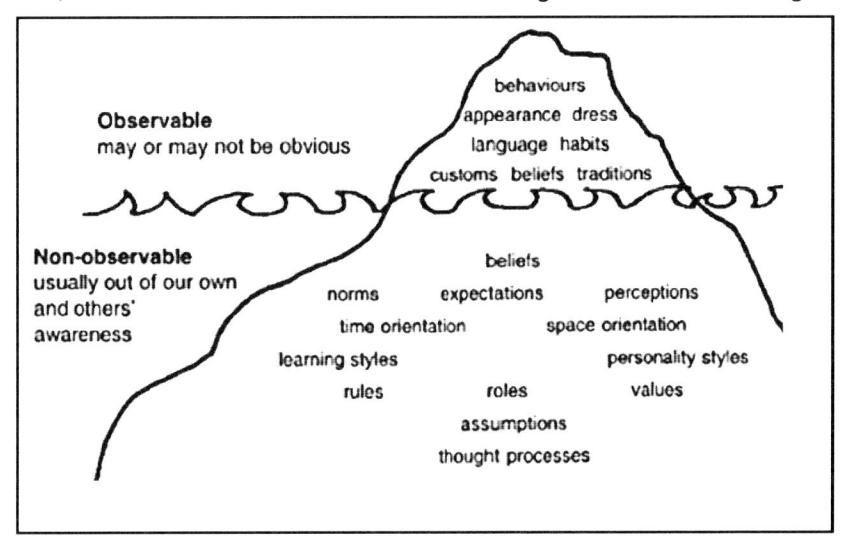

FIGURE 1: THE 'ICEBERG' MODEL OF CULTURE
(Source: Brisbane Catholic Education, 1998, p. 4)

The visible part of an iceberg is only a small fraction of the whole and by seeing only the tip of the iceberg, the danger of clashing with the hidden part under water, which contains about 80% of the iceberg, is fatal (Peterson, 2004). Ignoring this hidden part can mean cross-cultural clashes for mergers, acquisitions, alliances, joint ventures or any transactions across national borders (Hofstede *et al.*, 2010). The visible and observable culture elements contain behaviour, appearance, dress, language, habits, customs, and traditions. These cultural elements are obvious and are recognised very quickly (Peterson, 2004). But to understand these obvious elements, one has to look beyond the surface, as the invisible hidden elements are the cause and influence for the visible elements (Brett, 2007). Norms, beliefs, expectations, values, roles, assumptions, perceptions, time orientation, space orientation, learning styles, personality styles, rules, thought processes contain the hidden origins of culture and the core of it. As Brett (2007, p.27) states that 'there is more to culture below the surface, and just like an iceberg, culture is not static, it drifts and shifts'. This is only half of the truth, as Wederspahn (2000) argues that the surface factors of culture can change over time, as due to globalisation and trends people change their appearance, dress, habits, behaviour, *etc.*, but the 'deep culture' stays static and will not change rapidly overnight (Wederspahn, 2000). Peterson (2004, p.28) agrees to this point of view, as superficial cultural changes happen all over the world daily, whereas culture also 'maintain certain traits over decades and centuries'. Hofstede *et al.* (2010) describes the shifting modern world as only affecting the level of practice, which subsumes the manifestations of symbols, heroes and rituals and are visible to outside observers. However, their cultural meaning is invisible and lies only in the interpretation of the insider.

Figure 2 shows Hofstede's (2001) 'Onion of manifestations of culture'. While globalisation is only affecting the practices of culture like symbols in the way of people dress the same, buy the same products or use the same fashionable words, or heroes become globally accepted through television shows and movies or further rituals of engagement in the same sports and leisure activities, makes the world look as if it is becoming more similar. Nevertheless, the core of culture and the deeper, underlying level of values that determine the meaning of the practices for the people are manifested deep in the individual and will not change overnight due to a new trend or fashion (Hofstede *et al.*, 2010; Hoecklin, 1995). Hofstede *et al.* (1990, p.312) further state 'by the time a child is ten, most of his or her basic values are probably programmed into his or her mind' and will presumably not change throughout their life.

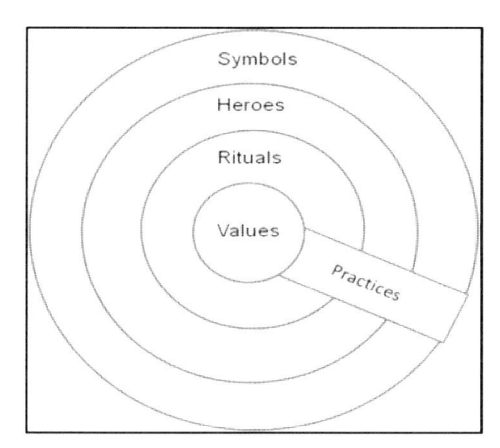

FIGURE 2: THE 'ONION DIAGRAM': MANIFESTATIONS OF CULTURE AT DIFFERENT LEVELS OF DEPTH.
(Source: Hofstede, 2001, p. 11)

Furthermore, it is agreed among researchers that culture consists of further several layers extended to Hofstede's (2001) assumptions, which can be visualised as an onion as well in the form of three layers: basic assumptions, norms and values, and artifacts and products (Schein, 2010).

Although different researchers have slightly different explanations of the deeper levels of culture, they do agree on certain characteristics. First, culture is a multilayer construct, and the deeper one digs into a culture, the more difficult it becomes to understand it. Furthermore, they do agree that culture is difficult to change, and again, the deeper the level of culture, the more difficult it is to change or influence it. Hofstede (1983), for example, explains that especially the onion's core, the basic assumptions are difficult to change as they are already shaped early in a child's life and constantly reinforced throughout life. However, artifacts and products, like Hofstede *et al.* (2010) explains, can change faster as the outer layer is influenced by the external environment and shapes the external reality.

Culture has been studied for a long time by researchers from diverse fields, but only recently culture is used to understand different behaviours of people in different countries within an organisational context (Francesco and Gold, 2005).

2.1.1 National culture

National culture is the broadest level of culture a person can be a member of. It shapes people from early childhood through values, beliefs-, and assumptions inherent in it (Hofstede, 1991). Moreover, national culture is a learned characteristic and none of it is genetic (Hofstede, 2007). While Kogut and Singh (1988) simply define national cultural distance as the degree to which norms are different between countries, Hofstede (1983) suggests that there are three reasons for the existence of differences among countries: political, sociological and psychological. 'Nations are political units, rooted in history, with their own institutions: forms of government, legal systems, educational systems, labor and employer's association systems' (Hofstede, 1983, p.75). Obviously formal institutions differ, but even though one would try to match the political units of different countries, the informal way of the implementation would still differ. A further attribute that distinguishes countries is sociology. Belonging to a nation has a symbolic value to citizens and shapes a part of the identity. This sense of identity creates a common national identity, which citizens try to protect and defend if they have the feeling of threat. Lastly, Hofstede mentions psychological reasons for national cultural distance between countries. People's thinking is determined by national culture factors and the effect of early life experience and educational experiences whilst growing up (Hofstede, 1983).

Moreover, Lewis (1996, p.8) states, that 'comparisons of National cultures often begins by highlighting differences in social behaviour' and as Gooderham and Nordhaug (2001) add that individuals become aware of their own culture when they are confronted with another.

2.1.2 Organisational culture

'Organisations, like nations, have cultures' (Francesco and Gold, 2005). It is a pattern of basic assumptions as well and is invented, discovered or developed by a given group of people while coping with problems of internal integration and external adaption. This way of doing things and coping with problems has worked well enough to be considered valid and thus is taught as the correct way of doing things to new members (Schein, 1985). Therefore, organisational culture is seen as the 'natural' way of understanding the business world and taking action (Francesco and Gold, 2005).

Moreover, Hofstede *et al.* (2010) explicate that organisational culture consists of the following attributes: holistic, historically determined, related to the things anthropologists study, socially constructed, soft and difficult to change, and further applies his definition of culture to organisational culture: 'the collective programming of the mind that distinguishes the members of one organization from others' (Hofstede *et al.*, 2010, p.344).

Besides, Armstrong (2003) states, that while national culture is impossible to change, organisational culture can be changed within the fractious process of change management. While national culture is shaped during the early childhood, organisational culture is learned and adopted while entering the employment market and gaining work experience (Hofstede *et al.*, 2010). The organisational culture is not as deeply rooted as national culture and even though resistance is usually very high during change management processes, the capability to change is given.

Furthermore, Martin (1992, p.113) argues that the national culture is influencing the organisational culture immensely and that 'we cannot understand what goes on inside an organizational culture without understanding what exists outside the boundaries'.

2.2 HOFSTEDE'S STUDY OF CULTURAL DIMENSIONS

Geert Hofstede, a Dutch social psychologist, published his landmark study in 1980 "*Cultures Consequences: International Differences in Work related Values*" (Hofstede, 1980). Through his cross-cultural studies he identified four main dimensions, later six, which affect human thinking, organisations, and institutions in predictable ways (Francesco and Gold, 2003). 'A dimension is an aspect of a culture that can be measured relative to other cultures' (Hofstede *et al.*, 2010, p.30). Moreover, Levitin (1973, p.492) states that dimensions are not tangible and that they are 'not directly accessible to observation but inferable from verbal statements and other behaviors and useful in predicting still other observable and measurable verbal and nonverbal behavior'. Furthermore, Hofstede's (1980) research had a remarkable effect on academics and practitioners (Jones, 2007) and was cited and utilised in a wide range of social context, is taught in class rooms and subject in organisational training (Dawson and Young, 2003) and is further the most cited Non-American in the US Social Science Citation Index (Powell, 2006). Hofstede's study of pioneering character based on a huge amount of data was taken up enthusiastically by many researchers and has been accepted and adopted quickly within academic and organisational environment ever since.

In his book, Hofstede (1980) identified four dimensions (later on six) for 40 countries to discover cultural differences. These four dimensions are: Power Distance (PD), Uncertainty Avoidance (UA), Individualism/ Collectivism (IDV), Masculinity/Femininity (MAS), added later on by Long-term Orientation (LTO) and recently Indulgence vs. Restraint. These dimensions are further compared with national measurements, such as Gross National Product (GNP), economic growth latitude, population size, population growth, population density and organisation size (Hofstede, 2001).

2.2.1 Research data

Hofstede's (1980) book is based on the largest survey of value works in the multinational company of International Business Machines (IBM), which was held twice, in 1967 and in 1973 (Hofstede, 1980). At that time, IBM was one of the largest multinational companies with numerous subsidiaries in many different countries around the world and sold a wide range of high-technology products for particular computers (Data Processing Division) and typewriters (Office Products Division). In the duration of the data collection IBM had research laboratories in two countries, developed its products in seven countries, manufactured in thirteen countries and marketed and serviced in about one hundred countries (Hofstede, 2001). Geert Hofstede was hired by IBM in 1965 as the first personnel researcher for the European head office to conduct an international employee morale survey. Hofstede and his team of six researchers prepared the first internationally standardized questionnaire for a simultaneous survey, which consisted of 180 standardized items. During that time conducting an international survey was facing distribution problems as the internet was not yet well established and questionnaires needed to be filled out manually and sent via post back to the headquarter. Issues, such as missing, stolen or lost questionnaires were not uncommon (ibid).

Over these six years, Hofstede and his colleagues collected and analysed 117,000 questionnaires of IBM employees in 53 and later in 72 countries all over the world, from which over 88,000 people responded (Hofstede, 1980; Hofstede, 2001; Jones, 2007; Powell, 2006). IBM's international employee attitude survey program was carried out between 1967 and 1973 with the purpose of identifying preferences in specific areas of employee morale and attitude (French, 2010; Hofstede, 2001). A factor analysis of 32 questions in 40 countries was made from the obtained data. Four bipolar dimensions emerged from that and became the basis of his characterisations of culture for each country (Jones, 2007). The first study was limited to 40 countries due to low response rates in some countries. A minimum of 50 respondents needed to be ensured for a reasonable result (Hofstede, 2001).

From 1971 to 1973 Hofstede taught organisational behaviour at the IMEDE Management Development Institute in Lausanne, Switzerland, a postgraduate and post experience international business school. Using the IBM questionnaire as teaching material he decided to administer a reduced version of the IBM survey and obtained data from 362 managers from 30 different countries. It provided the first hard proof for Hofstede that the differences within the IBM study was not company but country specific (Hofstede, 2001; Hofstede *et al.*, 2010).

2.2.2 Cultural dimensions

In the following section Hofstede's (2001) cultural dimensions are described and analysed in detail. The specific indices are shown in Appendix A.

Power Distance (PD): is defined by Hofstede *et al.* (2010, p.61) as 'the extent to which less powerful members of institutions and organizations within a country expect and accept that power is distributed unequally'; where institutions are seen as the basic elements of society, such as family, school and the community and organisations are the people's work places (ibid). Mullins (2007, p.25) adds, that PD 'is used to categorise levels of inequality in organisations, which Hofstede claims depend upon management style, willingness of subordinates to disagree with superiors, and the educational level and status accruing to particular roles'. Furthermore, PD represents a society's level of inequality which is admitted as much as by followers as by leaders. Inequality and power are two fundamental facts of a society and considering international comparison it is obvious that all societies are unequal, but some might be more unequal than others (Hofstede and Hofstede, 2009a).

However, Fougere and Moulettes (2006) criticise Hofstede for evaluating the Power Distance Index (PDI) and distinguishing between 'low PDI' as 'modern' and 'high PDI' as 'traditional'. They state that Hofstede suggests from his western point of view, the 'low PDI' side as better than the other, as this side is deemed to be more technological, more legal, modern, educated, wealthy, fair, equal, democratic, *etc.*. Nevertheless, Hofstede states in Powell (2006) that there is no such thing as better or worse score within the indices, that the scores are treated completely neutral and there are no assumed disadvantages of being on one side or the other.

Individualism/ Collectivism (IDV): The Individualism Index (IDV) represents the relatively individualistic or collectivist ethic evident in a particular society (Mullins, 2007). Additionally, Hofstede and de Mooij (2010, p.88/89) define Individualism/ Collectivism as 'people looking after themselves and their immediate family only, versus people belonging to in-groups that look after them in exchange for loyalty'. Moreover, they state that individualistic cultures are universalistic in assuming that their values are valid for the whole world and are low-communication cultures with explicit verbal communication. In contrast, in collectivistic cultures an individual's identity is based on the society and avoiding loss of face is important. Additionally, collectivistic cultures are high-context communication cultures, as these cultures use an indirect style of communication. Konopaske and Ivancevich (2004) characterise individualistic individuals as being motivated by the self-concept, self-ego and self-interest and collectivistic individuals as group oriented and with a higher awareness of the group's interest rather than the individual's.

While Hofstede (2001) claims that the dimensions are bi-polar and the dimensions are composed of contrasting poles, individualism is treated as the opposite pole of collectivism. Triandis (1994) however, argues that these dimensions can coexist and are depending more or less on the situation.

Masculinity/ Femininity (MAS): 'Masculinity versus its opposite, femininity refers to the distribution of roles between the genders which is another fundamental issue for any society to which a range of solutions are found' (Hofstede and Hofstede, 2009a). In masculine societies 'the tough values- including success, money assertiveness, and competition- are dominant' (Francesco and Gold, 2005, p.27). While in feminine cultures the importance lies on tender values, such as quality for life, personal relationship, care for others, and service (ibid). This dimension does not refer to the dominance of the gender, but more the degree to which masculine traits or feminine characteristics are given (Jones, 2007). Hofstede *et al.* (2010) distinguish between the masculine and feminine pole, where the importance of earnings, recognition, advancement and challenge are creating the masculine pole and, on the other hand good relationship with the manager, cooperation, living area and employment security the feminine pole. Role differentiation is an important aspect of this dimension, as it is small in feminine societies and large in masculines. In feminine countries, for example household work is more shared between husband and wife than in masculine countries (Hofstede and de Mooij, 2010).

The MAS dimension has probably aroused the most criticism over the years and is blamed for being vague and contradictory. For instance, its lack of meaning and its gender role differentiation- is criticised by Fougere and Moulettes (2006). However, Hofstede (2001) claims that the many scholars who have misinterpreted this dimension do not accept the convergence in social gender roles.

Uncertainty Avoidance (UA): Uncertainty Avoidance (UA) is defined by Hofstede *et al.* (2010, p.191) as 'the extent to which the members of a culture feel threatened by ambiguous or unknown situations'. This is expressed through a need for predictability and through nervous stress (Hofstede *et al.*, 2010). Individuals in high UA cultures feel threatened by risky and uncertain situations and are constantly trying to minimize risk and uncertainty by developing strict laws and rules or formal regulations (Konopaske and Ivancevich, 2004). Strong UA is shown in a need for security and strict rules and structure, which can hinder change and innovation. Weak UA is represented through unstructured situations, more flexible and more easy-going. In this environment changes and innovations, as well as entrepreneurial spirit are more welcomed (Francesco and Gold, 2005). This aspect is criticised by Shane (1993) as he states, that low UA countries had shown a high rate of innovation in terms of trademarks granted. Nevertheless, Hofstede *et al.* (2010) claims that only the dimension's extremes are described and that countries usually are not presenting an extreme but are positioned more in the middle. Moreover, McSweeney (2002) state that the question for measuring the index about 'rules should not be broken' is critical, as the meaning can differ from country to country, especially as the question leaves too much room for subjective interpretation.

Long-term orientation (LTO): 'Long- versus short-term orientation is the extent to which a society exhibits a pragmatic future-oriented perspective rather than a conventional historic short-term point of view' (Hofstede and de Mooij, 2010, p.90). This fifth dimension, which was originally named 'Confucian work dynamism', was developed by Michael Bond, whose attempt was to identify Chinese cultural values and their impact on the workplace (Mullins, 2007). With the 'Chinese Value Survey' (CVS) Michael Bond and a number of his Chinese colleagues from Hong Kong and Taiwan created a non-westernised survey. As Hofstede and Bond were interested in new methods and tools, which were not created in their so called 'Western world' and influenced by western values, the CVS offered them a new point of view from a different angle (Hofstede *et al.*, 2010). The CVS was administered to one hundred university students in twenty-three different countries around the world. The resulted factor-analysis demonstrated four extracted factors, where three of them correlated with Hofstede's cultural dimensions (Wu, 2006). Only UA did not have an equivalent in the CVS. The emerged fourth CVS dimension combined values opposing a future orientation versus past and present orientation (Hofstede, 2001). This dimension was called 'Confucian Work Dynamic' and included four items: 1. Ordering relationship; 2. Thrift; 3. Persistence; and 4. Having a sense of shame. These Confucian values in the Chinese society as an eastern cultural dimension was adopted by Hofstede and renamed into 'Long-term orientation' (Wu, 2006).

Hofstede *et al.* (2010, p.239) defines long-term orientation as 'the fostering of virtues oriented toward future rewards- in particular, perseverance and thrift'. Short-term orientation is thereafter 'the fostering of virtues related to the past and present- in particular, respect for tradition, preservation of 'face', and fulfilling social obligations'. The scores for LTO were recalculated and further countries could be added to the index in the newest edition of Hofstede's book 'Cultures and Organizations: Software of the mind' (2010) with the help of the new Co-author Misho Minkov.

After the success of the eastern cultural dimension, Hofstede considered to go further and tried to adopt this approach to Africa with the possibility of an emergent African value dimension (Hofstede, 2001). Even though six factors were produced and five of them correlated with the previous dimensions, the remaining factor 'was no serious candidate for a new, African-inspired, cultural dimension' (Hofstede, 2001, p.370). This is heavily criticised by Fougere and Moulettes (2006) as they argue that Hofstede thinks that Africa is not worth its own dimension. However, the evidence for creating a new African dimension was not enough and further researches needed to be done before considering a valid and reliable new dimension.

Indulgence vs. Restraint (IVR): In the last edition of Hofstede's book 'Cultures and Organizations: Software of the mind' (2010) with the Co-authors Geert Jan Hofstede and Misho Minkov this new dimension was added: Indulgence versus Restraint. By re-analysing the enormous data of the World Value Survey (WVS), which is a global survey administered in more than one hundred countries and including more than 360 forced-choice items, Minkov extracted three dimensions. He named these dimension: exclusionism vs. universalism, which correlated with collectivism vs. individualism; indulgence vs. restraint and monumentalism vs. flexhumility, which correlated significantly with short- vs. long-term orientation. The analysis of the latter resulted in a new measurement of the LTO dimension and an enriched understanding of its implications and an increasing number of included countries (Hofstede et al., 2010).

The new emerged dimension, Indulgence versus Restraint, is focusing on happiness and life control. Indulgence 'stands for a society that allows relatively free gratification and natural human drives related to enjoying life and having fun' (Hofstede et al., 2010, p.281). Whereas, restraint reflects a society, which suppresses gratifications of needs, by regulating it with means of strict social norms (Hofstede and Hofstede, 2009a). People from indulgent societies are more likely to remember positive emotions, have less moral disciplines, have more extrovert personalities, have higher optimism and leisure time and having friends is very important. Individuals in restraint societies are less likely to remember positive emotions, leisure time and friends are less important, cynicism and moral discipline are stronger and people are more pessimistic (Hofstede et al., 2010).

Due to the recent publications and release of this new dimension, no critique or comments are available so far and Hofstede et al. (2010) state, that this dimension needs more study and further in-depth analyses.

2.2.3 Other cultural studies and comparison with Hofstede's dimensions

French (2010) states, that Hofstede is the pioneer of cross-cultural study and the most influential organisational sociologist. Moreover, Hoecklin (1995) praises his pioneering work, and Powell (2006) claims that Hofstede created a milestone of cultural study and a driving force for other researchers to continue researching about culture.

However, there are several other influential and important studies about culture by Trompenaar, Schwartz, Kluckhohn and Strodtbeck, Hall and Hall, and recently the GLOBE project. These studies deepen the study of culture by making it more feasible and understandable. Hofstede (2001) states, that about 200 external comparative studies support the cultural differences measured by his indices. The most important ones, are the one stated above, which Hofstede uses within his book to support his dimensions. Each study correlates with some of the identified cultural dimensions, but none of them, except of the GLOBE project, which is built on Hofstede's framework, included all dimensions. A comparison of Hofstede's dimensions and other cultural studies is shown in Figure 3 below:

Hofstede's five Cultural Dimensions

Power Distance	Individualism/ Collectivism	Masculinity/ Femininity	Uncertainty Avoidance	Long-term orientation	Indulgence vs. Restraint
- Trompenaar - GLOBE	- Kluckhohn/ Strodtbeck - Hall/ Hall - Trompenaar - Schwartz - GLOBE	- GLOBE	- GLOBE	- Kluckhohn/ Strodtbeck - Hall/ Hall - Trompenaar - Schwartz - GLOBE	- Trompenaar - GLOBE

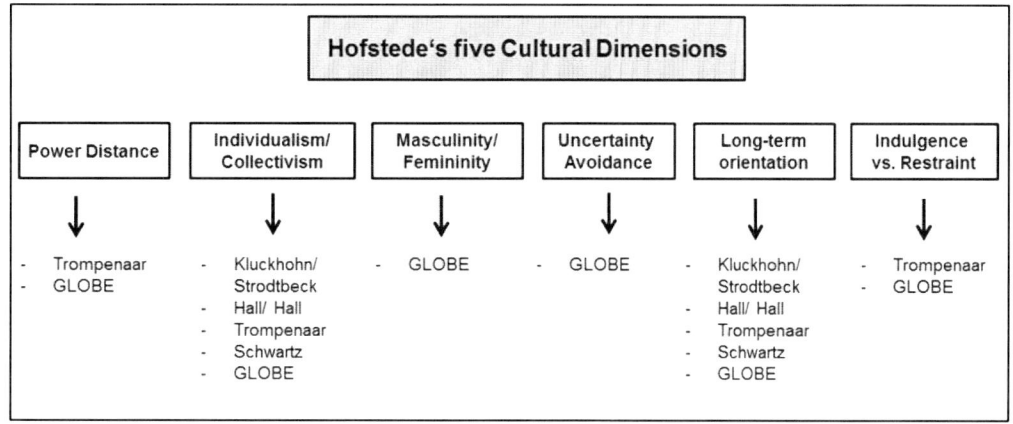

FIGURE 3: COMPARISON OF HOFSTEDE'S CULTURAL DIMENSION WITH OTHER CULTURAL STUDIES
(Source: Own Illustration based on Neumann, 2008, p.5; Carr, 2004, p.24; Francesco and Gold, 2005, pp.20-33; Hoecklin, 1995, pp.27-46; Trompenaar and Hampden-Turner, 1997, p.8/9; Konopaske and Ivancevich, 2004, pp.32-35)

In the following section the main cultural studies are discussed briefly and the similarities of cultural differences with Hofstede's (1980) dimensions are pointed out.

Trompenaar: Beside Hofstede, Trompenaar's study on national culture differences is probably the second most popular study of cultural differences. Trompenaar and Hampden-Turner (1997) surveyed 15,000 managers from 28 nations and received around 500 valid responses from each country and developed seven dimensions on which culture diverge. Of those dimensions, five are used to describe how people deal with each other, while the other two refer to the concepts of time and environment (Warner and Joynt, 2003). The seven dimensions are:

TABLE I:
TROMPENAARS 7 DIMENSIONS

1. Universalism vs. Particularism	societal versus personal obligation
2. Specific vs. Diffuse	degree of involvement in relationships
3. Individualism vs. Communitarianism	personal versus group goals
4. Affective vs. Neutral	emotional orientation in relationships
5. Achievement vs. Ascription	legitimation of power and status
6. Sequential vs. Synchronous	time orientation
7. Internal vs. External control	relation to nature

(Source: Hoecklin, 1995; Trompenaar and Hampden-Turner, 1997)

Several of those dimensions have overlaps with some of Hofstede's cultural dimension. Individualism versus Communitarianism relates to Individualism versus Collectivism, Achievement versus Ascription to Power Distance and Sequential versus Synchronous to Long-term orientation. However, Hofstede (1996) criticised Trompenaar's study for being cultural biased and questioned the representativeness of his study.

Schwartz: Shalom Schwartz, an Israeli psychologist concentrates on universal aspects of individual value content and structure. The dimensions of Schwartz are based on three issues all societies are confronted with: '(1) the nature of the relation or boundaries between the individual and the group, (2) how to guarantee responsible behaviour, and (3) how to regulate the relation of people to the natural and social world' (Francesco and Gold, 2005, p.30). Over ten years, Schwartz collected data from over 60,000 people in 63 countries, where most of the respondents were teachers at universities and schools (Sagiv and Schwartz, 2000). From the results, Schwartz developed three bipolar dimensions of culture, which shows different solutions to the issues that confront societies (Schwartz, 1992). These dimensions are:

TABLE II:

SCHWARTZ'S DIMENSIONS

1. Embeddedness versus Autonomy	People as part of a collective vs. individuals as autonomous
2. Hierarchy versus Egalitarianism	Unequal distribution of power vs. recognition of people as moral equals
3. Mastery versus Harmony	Exploitation of the natural or social environment vs. fitting in harmoniously with the environment

(Source: Francesco and Gold, 2005; Thomas and Inkson, 2003; Schwartz, 1992)

The first dimension of Embeddedness versus Autonomy relates to Individualism vs. Collectivism and Mastery versus Harmony relates to Short-/Long-term orientation (Neumann, 2008). Triandis (2004) suggests that the dimension of Hierarchy versus Egalitarianism refers to Power Distance if Individualism/ Collectivism seen as vertical or horizontal, but Neumann (2008) claims that Harmony correlates positively with Uncertainty Avoidance which makes it unclear of its suitability as Power Distance.

Kluckhohn and Strodtbeck: Kluckhohn and Strodtbeck (1961), two anthropologists, focused within their pioneering study not on the realm of work but on culture more generally. Their Values Orientation theory is based on three assumptions, namely that there are limited number of common human problems for which all people have to find solutions, that these solutions are limited in number and universally known, and that different cultures have different preferences among those solutions (Kluckhohn and Strodtbeck, 1961). They developed the following dimensions:

TABLE III:

KLUCKHOHN'S AND STRODTBECK'S DIMENSION

1. Relation to nature	subjugation, harmony or mastery
2. Time orientation	past, present or future
3. Basic human nature	evil, neutral, good
4. Activity orientation	being, controlling, doing
5. Relationship among people	individualistic, group or hierarchy
6. Space orientation	private, mixed or public

(Source: Konopaske and Ivancevich, 2004)

The second dimension is similar to Short- and Long-term orientation and the dimension of 'Relationship among others' can be referred to Individualism/ Collectivism.

Hall and Hall: The American anthropologist, Edward T. Hall (1976) explains the differences in communication styles among cultures with the concept of context. 'Context is the information that surrounds an event; it is inextricably bound up with the meaning of that event' (Hall and Hall, 1989, p.64). These can be divided into:

TABLE IV:

HALL AND HALL COMMUNICATION STYLES

1. High context	implicit and indirect communication style
2. Low context	direct communication style

(Source: French, 2010; Francesco and Gold, 2005)

Moreover, Hall (1976) developed the concept of monochronic versus polychronic time orientation:

TABLE V:

HALL AND HALL TIME ORIENTATION

3. Monochronic	people preferring to do one task at a time
4. Polychronic	people can handle many tasks simultaneously

(Source: Hofstede and de Mooij, 2010)

While High- and low-context are characteristics of Collectivism and Individualism, the aspect of time orientation is related according to Neumann (2004) to short-/ long-term orientation. Even though the understanding of the word 'time' is basically different, the basic assumption is the same.

GLOBE project: The 'Global Leadership and Organizational Behaviour Effectiveness' research project (GLOBE) reports the result of a ten-year research program and is designed to conceptualize, operationalize, test, and validate a cross-level integrated theory of the relationship between culture, societal, organisational and leadership effectiveness. 170 investigators from 62 cultures are working on this project and obtained data from 17,300 managers in 951 organisations (House *et al*, 2004). The third round of obtaining data from over 17,000 managers is taking place right now in the year 2010/2011 (Hofstede *et al*, 2010). The origins and foundations of the GLOBE approach are derived from the models and dimensions described above (House *et al.*, 2004; Hofstede, 2006). The GLOBE dimensions mainly adopted Hofstede's (1980) cultural dimensions, and hence identified the following dimensions out of their huge amount of data:

TABLE VI:

GLOBE DIMENSIONS

1. Power Distance	extent to which power is expected to be equally distributed
2. Uncertainty Avoidance	extent to which individuals try to avoid and prevent uncertain events
3. Humane Orientation	degree to which a collective encourages and rewards individuals for being fair and generous
4. Collectivism I (Institutional Collectivism)	degree to which organisational and societal institutional practices encourage and reward collective distribution of resources and collective action
5. Collectivism II (In-Group Collectivism)	(degree to which an individual is bonded with, and is loyal to a sub-societal group such as family or work organisation
6. Assertiveness	degree to which an individual is assertive, confrontational and aggressive in their relationship to others
7. Gender Egalitarianism	degree to which gender inequality is handled
8. Future Orientation	extent to which individuals are engaged in future-oriented behaviours
9. Performance Orientation	degree to which a collective rewards and encourages individuals for performance improvement and excellence

(Source: French, 2010; House *et al.*, 2004)

These nine dimensions were developed out of 78 survey questions, where half of the questions were asking about their culture 'as it is' and the other half of the questions were asking about the 'as it should be'. Thus, nine dimensions for each orientation were developed resulting in 18 dimensions (Hofstede *et al.*, 2010). The GLOBE project is the most contemporary mammoth survey nowadays and is expanding Hofstede's approach of cultural dimensions by the contribution of 170 investigators from 62 cultures, which secures the non-cultural bias (French, 2010). However, Hofstede *et al.* (2010, p.42) criticize the GLOBE project 'for having formulated the questions in researchers' jargon, not reflective of the problems on the responding (mainly first-line) managers' minds' and further for ignoring personal desires. Hofstede (2006, p.884) calls it a 'debatable approach' as he doubts the representation of the real picture by asking managers and hence he questions the validity.

Summary: While Hofstede's (1980) study provided a breakthrough in the analysis of national cultural differences, the other researchers support the findings and further extend his work. Although the authors tend to criticize each other's model or the research procedure, the models complement each other and increase the literature's value. Moreover, there is not only one best approach of studying culture and cultural differences, as there are many ways of doing so especially when considering the number of different culture definitions (Warner and Joynt, 2003). For each and every model of cultural identification aroused praise and criticism and therefore made culture discussable and nameable. Table VII illustrates the most important cultural studies and their matching of dimensions and differences.

TABLE VII:

COMPARISON OF CULTURAL STUDIES

Hofstede	Kluckhohn/ Strodtbeck	Hall/ Hall	Trompenaar	GLOBE
Individualism vs. Collectivism	Relationship among people	'high-context' vs. 'low-context'	Individualism vs. Collectivism	Individualism Group pride
	Activity Orientation		Achieved vs. Fixed status	
Power Distance			Similarity vs. Hierarchy	Power Distance
	Relation to nature		Inner vs. External control	
			Universalism vs. Particularism	Humaneness
	Basic Human Nature			
Short- vs. long term orientation	Time Orientation	Monochronic vs. Polychronic	Sequential vs. Synchronous time	Future Orientation
Uncertainty Avoidance				Uncertainty Avoidance
Masculinity vs. Femininity				Gender differentiation
Indulgence vs. Restraint			Specificity vs. Diffusion	Performance orientation
			Affective vs. Neutral	

(Source: Own Illustration based on Neumann, 2008, p.18; Carr, 2004, p.24; Francesco and Gold, 2005, pp.20-33; Hoecklin, 1995, pp.27-46; Trompenaar and Hampden-Turner, 1997, p.8/9; Konopaske and Ivancevich, 2004, pp.32-35)

Resulting from Table VII, it is obvious that Hofstede's (2001) cultural dimensions have got always one or more counterparts in several other studies and especially GLOBE is supporting every single dimension of Hofstede and even adding further ones. Thus, GLOBE can be seen as the contemporary, intensified and broader version of Hofstede's cultural dimension. However, the appliance is not as simple as Hofstede's and the huge amount of data and in total eighteen cultural dimensions are making its practical use even more difficult. The most significant culture dimensions with the most matching counterparts are the dimensions of Individualism versus Collectivism and Long-term versus Short-term orientation.

2.3 ANALYSIS AND EVALUATION OF HOFSTEDE'S FINDINGS

'Geert Hofstede is one of the most significant contributors to the body of knowledge on culture and workplace difference' (Mullins, 2007, p.24). Further, his research has been instrumental in understanding cross-cultural management theory and practice (Fernandez et al., 1997).

However, over the last 40 years many authors have criticised Hofstede's (1980) concept of cultural differences and challenged it by publishing critical journal articles (Jones, 2007; Nakata, 2009; McSweeney, 2002; Moulettes, 2007; Søndergaard, 2010; etc.). Hofstede (2001) is aware of the criticism that occurs around his cultural study and used the opportunity of his second book to address the main criticisms.

Hofstede (1980) as any other great social scientist like Keynes, Malthus or Philips has got his protagonists as well as antagonists. This section aims to analyse and critically evaluate the main arguments in support of Hofstede and against him, which are shown in the table below:

TABLE VIII:

ARGUMENTS FOR AND AGAINST HOFSTEDE'S STUDY

Arguments for Hofstede (1980)	Arguments against Hofstede (1980)
Relevance	Reliability and Validity of Methodology
Rigour	One Company Approach
Relative Accuracy	National Divisions
Simplicity	Political Influences
	Out-dated
	Too few dimensions
	Culturally biased
	Ecological Fallacy

(Source: Own illustration)

2.3.1 Arguments in support of Hofstede's study

The success and popularity of Hofstede's cultural dimensions are explained by Nakata (2009), as the uniqueness of this mammoth survey, which indicates thousands of respondents in a diverse array of countries and regions and allows a wide range of adaptions. This is only one of the several aspects that are supporting Hofstede's study. More arguments for Hofstede's model are discussed below.

Relevance: Jones (2007) states, that during the time of Hofstede's discoveries, there was little work on culture and especially in this time many companies were just globalising and entering the international arena and the need for cultural explanations was tremendous (Nakata, 2009). Therefore his explorations came at the right time and the right place, as Gladwell (2008) explains the timing is one main important external factor of succeeding popularity and recognition. Hofstede's work represented guidance for managers in expanding businesses, as clashing cultures were making business difficult (Hofstede *et al.*, 2010). Furthermore, Søndergaard (1994) states that Hofstede was seen as a pathfinder and pioneer, by drawing attention to the importance of culture and making it more feasible and discussable.

Rigour: The research framework, which was used by Hofstede, is stated to be a rigorous design with a systematic data collection and a coherent theory (Jones, 2007). The marketplace and scholars needed such a framework with a broad and unique explanation of cultural differences. Such a mammoth survey with more than a hundred thousand respondents gave an insight into culture that had not been available before (Nakata, 2009). Several authors used Hofstede's framework to further analyse culture and to replicate his study.

Relative Accuracy: The accuracy of Hofstede's dimensions and the relevancy of the questions he used, was tested and replicated by several researchers and studies (Søndergaard, 1994). As shown in the previous section, most of Hofstede's dimensions are supported by several other authors and especially Individualism/ Collectivism and Long-term orientation are widely supported by other researchers. Further, Hofstede (2001) states himself that about 200 comparative studies supports the cultural differences and the dimensions, which further underlines the representativeness. Moreover, his framework is seen as the dominant culture paradigm in business studies and is the most widely cited theory in the Social Sciences Citation Index compared to competing ones (Nakata, 2009). The dimensions paradigm has become the 'normal science' approach to cross-cultural business studies and every researcher that attempts to analyse culture has to come across Hofstede and his work and would realise its importance (Kuhn, 1970).

Simplicity: Knudsen and Loloma (2007) argue that the immense success of Hofstede's framework is due to its simplicity of appliance. The complexity of culture is reduced by quantifiable and comparable cultural dimensions, which is easily applied to various intercultural encounters. Hofstede (2001) offered managers, researchers and any individual who is interested in cultural differences a simple way of identifying and handling cultural differences. The six dimensions and their score indices make individuals understand and aware of cultural differences and without expert knowledge, intelligent lay readership can understand the basic assumptions and use the indices for their own purpose (Hofstede *et al.*, 2010; Jones, 2007).

2.3.2 Arguments against Hofstede's study

Since Hofstede published his landmark study of the cultural dimensions, several authors and researches have criticised his study and outlined the importance for a new understanding of culture (Baskerville, 2003; Jones, 2007; Nakata, 2009; McSweeney, 2002; Moulettes, 2007; Søndergaard, 2010; *etc.*). Some authors have just concentrated on criticising Hofstede's study, rather than creating or analysing further the broad topic of culture. The main critical point against Hofstede is that his concept might be out of date. Over the last 25 years the economies have become increasingly global and the growing industries and businesses change faster than ever (Blodgett, Bakir and Rose, 2008). The study of Hofstede had to face many criticisms and was reviewed several times, and Fougere and Moulettes (2006) argue that Hofstede's main purpose of the second edition of his book was mainly to address the criticism that his work has received in the previous years and to state that his work is still valid.

McSweeney (2002) is one of Hofstede's biggest critical antagonists, who published a critical article in 2002 about Hofstede's model of national cultural differences and called his work 'a triumph of faith- a failure of analysis'. Further criticism of Hofstede's study is mainly based on McSweeney's article on which Hofstede (2002) himself replied in the same issue of 'Human Relation'.

The main arguments discussed against Hofstede's study are analysed below.

Reliability and Validity of Methodology: The use of a 'survey' is discussed in the literature as not an appropriate instrument for determining and measuring cultural differences, especially when the measured variable is a culturally sensitive and subjective value (Schwartz, 1999). Baskerville (2003) and McSweeney (2002) argue that, culture is neither observable nor recordable or measurable and is therefore not captured by a questionnaire. Furthermore, Tayeb (1996) supports this view by criticising that an attitude-survey questionnaire is the least appropriate way of studying culture. Hofstede (2001, p.73) replied to this criticism, that 'they should not be the only way' and this was only one method to do so. Hofstede (2001) adds further that interviews and observations are obtaining more accurate data, but sample sizes tend to be very low as these methods are time and money consuming Further, Gooderham and Nordhaug (2001) support Hofstede's view, as they argue that a survey-based approach is highly efficient for comparing numerous countries. Even though self-reported questionnaires reduce the validity as problems occur such as differences in response style, translation, differences in interpretation, inability to handle incomprehensibility of questions or risk of filling out the questionnaire as groups, Taras and Steel (2009) still support Hofstede's choice of questionnaire method as every research strategy has got its advantages as well as disadvantages.

Moreover, McSweeney (2002) questions the representativeness of the result due to unequal and small respond rates. Only in six countries out of 72 the numbers of respondents was more than 1,000. Hofstede *et al.* (2008a) claims however, that 50 respondents is assumed to be a reliable result, but is also supplementary criticised by McSweeney (2002) as he doubts the representativeness of 50 respondents for a whole nation and further stated that 'the scale problem of Hofstede's research is radically compounded by the narrowness of the population surveyed' (McSweeney, 2002, p.96). The minimum number of respondents was 58 in Singapore (surveyed in 1971-73) and the maximum of 7,907 in Germany (surveyed in 1971-73) (Hofstede, 2001).

Besides, Dorfman and Howell (1988) identified several significant cross-loadings within the questionnaire, where 32 questions were observed with 40 cases or subjects. This could increase the chance of sample errors as cross-loadings endanger the validity of an item as its purpose is not clear. Thus the validity is further questioned by Myers and Tan (2002) and Baskerville (2003, 2005), as the data was not collected with the purpose in mind to identify cultural differences and cultural dimensions. Hofstede (2002, p.4) replies, that the first data set from the IBM survey was only the 'starting point of an exploration' and that the analysis of this data was the first attempt to identify cultural differences in precise measurements. To support his findings he tested data from other studies and correlated them with his findings, which mostly confirmed the dimensions.

Further, Hofstede *et al.* (2010) argues that protagonists failed to get the whole message of his study and as due to the huge amount of sudden data available, some lose track and tend to interpret the study wrongly.

Another criticism of the methodology is added by Warner and Joynt (2002) as they state that the dimensions are based on overall calculated mean score of individual respondents from several nations. However, a member of such a nation might not behave or correspond with such a calculated mean, which makes a generalisation questionable. Further, Taras and Steel (2009) claim that even though a mean provides essential information about a culture, it might not be appropriate to fully understand the phenomenon. Concentrating fully on mean scores might create a wrong perception of cultural homogeneity within a nation, due to considering of subcultures (Taras and Steel, 2009; French, 2010). McSweeney (2002, p.108) goes even further and states that 'what Hofstede 'identifies' is not national culture, but an averaging of situationally specific opinions from which dimensions or aspects, of national culture are unjustifiably inferred'. Hofstede (1980, p.45) calls the statistical average a 'national norm' and states 'we do not compare individuals, but we compare what is called central tendencies in the answers from each country. There is hardly an individual who answers each question exactly by the mean score of his or her group: the 'average person' from a country does not exist' (Hofstede, 1991, p.253).

One Company Approach: Even though the distribution location of the survey is a part of the methodology, the one company approach deserves a separate section due to its frequent mention in the criticism of several protagonists (McSweeney, 2002; Jones, 2007; Blodgett, Bakir and Rose, 2008). 'A study fixed on only one company cannot possibly provide information on the entire cultural system of a country' (Jones, 2007, p.5). Moreover, McSweeney (2002) argues that Hofstede's sample is not representative, because it is limited to one single company from mainly marketing and sales employees, which is supported by Robinson (1983) who states that middle-class employees could not represent a whole nation and the exclusion of unemployed individuals is criticised. This criticism is claimed by Hofstede (2001) as this is one of the main characteristics to compare the national samples as he is explaining in the VSM Manual 1994 and 2008 'comparisons of countries should be based on samples of respondents who are matched on all criteria, other than nationality, that could systematically affect the answers' (Hofstede *et al.*, 2008a, p.3). As the IBM data consisted of an unusually well matched and large sample of different countries, it could 'supply information about such differences' (Hofstede, 2001) between national cultures. Regarding this criticism, Hofstede *et al.* (2010) criticise the protagonists of his study for not doing appropriate research and lack of objectivity. However, McSweeney (2002, p.107) further argues that Hofstede analysed 'international differences in work-place values' with mainly work-related questions, but then makes conclusions about non work-related values. Hofstede (2001) makes the presupposition that culture is not situational specific within a nation.

Additionally, Baskerville (2003, 2005), Myers and Tan (2002), McSweeney (2002) and Gooderham and Nordhaug (2001), claim that the powerful US-derived organisational culture is influencing the outcome of the survey. But, Hofstede *et al.* (2010) states, that the values of employees cannot be changed by an organisation or employer, as they are learned and acquired when the employees were children and are deeply rooted in every individual.

National Divisions: 'Nations are not proper units of analysis as cultures are not necessarily bounded by borders' (Jones, 2007, p.5). Furthermore, Baskerville (2005) and Myers and Tan (2002) state, that nations do not have an own single and distinct culture and Nassif *et al.* (1991) add that most nations have subcultures and ethnic units. Questioning the cultural homogeneity of a nation is another frequent criticism, as Baskerville (2003) state that, for example in the Middle East the 'Human Relations Area Files' identifies 35 different cultures in 14 nations, in Africa 48 countries with 98 different cultures, in Western Europe 81 cultures in 32 countries. Wildavsky (1998) further argues, that cultures are not countries and that countries obtain several subcultures. Hofstede (2001, p.73) actually agrees to this point and states: 'True, but they are usually the only kind of units available for comparison and better than nothing'.

Political Influences: The timing of the survey may have been sensitive concerning the dimensions of Masculinity and Uncertainty Avoidance, as Europe was in the midst of the cold war and just recovering from World War II and similarly the communist insurgence in Asia. These political instabilities at that time could have influenced the outcome of the survey (Jones, 2007). Moreover, the sample lacks of data from third world countries as well as from socialist countries.

Out-dated: Many researchers have claimed that Hofstede's study is out-dated and too old to be of any modern value, especially in today's rapidly changing global environments (Jones, 2007; McSweeney, 2002; Baskerville, 2003). The almost 40 year old study might not be representative anymore and due to the 'global village' and the 'flattening world' the cultural dimensions might not be valid anymore. Further, Mullins (2007) argues that the questioned IBM employees might be dead already and criticises that their grandchildren might not have the same values. Hofstede (2001, p.34) on the other hand claims that 'cultures, especially national cultures, are extremely stable over time'. In contrast Myers and Tan (2002), McSweeney (2002), Baskerville (2005) argue that culture is highly dynamic and can shift over time and Scheuch (1996) actually proves the instability of culture, by measuring the results of 'attitude towards work' questions over a 30-year period in Germany.

Hofstede (2001, p.73) argues that 'the dimensions found are assumed to have centuries-old roots' and even if the practices have changed over time and symbols, heroes and rituals emerge globally, the values are deeply rooted and they determine the culture and cannot easily be changed (Hofstede, 2001). Hofstede and Hofstede (2009) claim that '[t]he forces that cause cultures to shift tend to be global or continent-wide - they affect many countries at the same time, so that if their cultures shift, they shift together, and their relative positions remain the same'. Especially the dimension of Individualism gains more attention over changing times, due to more independence and countries getting richer (Powell, 2006).

This is one of the main criticisms that occur around Hofstede's study and many replications were undertaken to evaluate the contemporary validity of his study. This study attempts to evaluate this contemporary validity by a replication study of two dimensions in two selected countries.

Too few dimensions: Five or now six dimensions are criticised as being not enough to explain the whole complexity of cultural differences (Baskerville, 2003). Hofstede (2001; 2002) states, that the work of cultural analysis is still unfinished and encourages further research as he claims that his cultural dimensions are not the only way and that further dimensions should be developed. However, the comprised cultural information within six dimensions offers a simple application and increases therefore its usability within the practice.

Culturally biased: Knudsen and Loloma (2007) outline the western bias of Hofstede's study as the dimensions are chosen from a westernised point of view. Gooderham and Nordhaug (2001) support this view, as they state that Hofstede is culturally biased due to the comprised European and American team. Hofstede is well aware of this point and states in his last edition (2010) that even the IBM questionnaire and people's way of thinking is culturally constrained. 'As the researchers were human, they were also children of their cultures' (Hofstede *et al.,* 2010, p.37) and the IBM survey was a western-minded product. Western questions were answered by non-western citizens. Therefore, Michael Bond tried to solve the western bias problem with the Chinese Value Survey (CVS), which was described in section 2.2.2.

Ecological Fallacy: Ecological Fallacy is described by French (2010, p.33) as a form of stereotyping which is further defined as 'cultural values which are known to be held by a group are projected onto an individual who is a member of the group'. Moreover, Taras and Steel (2009, p.47) describe this unwritten rule in the cross-cultural study field as 'Never Mix National and Individual Levels of Analysis'. Hofstede (2001) warns about this error of using the average tendencies to interpret on the individual level. However, he undertakes this error himself by telling stories about important people in history and referring back to the cultural dimensions and their characteristic behaviour (Neumann, 2009; McSweeney, 2002).

2.3.3 Discussion

Hofstede's (1980) study of cultural dimensions has gained a lot of attention, either supporting or criticising. However, it can be said that his study is well known to cultural researchers and has had a huge impact in the field of cultural studies. However, some researchers might have been too enthusiastically about the huge amount of data Hofstede obtained from so many countries that an agreement was quickly made and Hofstede's mammoth survey was quickly accepted and adopted.

Nevertheless, where there are supporting protagonists there are antagonists as well and Hofstede (1980; 2001) was not spared by criticism. Every incremental new theory is criticised and its validity is analysed, like the 'scientific revolution' fostered by Galileo Galilei who claimed that the sun was the centre of the universe and not the earth and eventually he was forced to recant for that (Finocchiaro, 2008).

The main criticism refers to the methodology Hofstede (1980) used and many authors questioned its validity and its reliability. Even though the body of criticism is growing, there is still continuing evidence of the durability of the study and 'there is no apparent sign of any waning of interest in Hofstede's research' (French, 2010, p.57). Moreover, Hoecklin (1995, p.48) states that 'there is no absolute right or wrong in cultural preferences' which is in accordance to Hofstede *et al.* (2010) who never stated that his way is the only way to study culture.

Even though the quantity of arguments against Hofstede's (1980) study is greater, the arguments supporting his study are assumed to outperform in quality. Resulting from the analysis of the literature, it can be said that Hofstede's (1980) study of cultural dimension is not perfect and has got its errors and shortcomings, but overall is a solid and reasonable study. However, his model should be used with caution and doubts to prevent misinterpretations and failure of application.

2.4 HOFSTEDE'S FINDINGS IN PRACTICE

The theory of Hofstede's (1980) study seems from the literature to be still solid and reasonable. But to what extent does the model of cultural dimensions add value to manager's everyday life and in which way is it of use and applicable in the practice?

The first step of effective cross-cultural management is the awareness of cultural differences and the need for understanding one's own culture and the host culture. Hofstede (1980) made people aware of existing cultural differences and the possibility that domestic strategies might fail in host countries. Therefore, appropriate training and teaching is necessary to gain multicultural interactive skills, cultural awareness as well as cultural intelligence. 'Cultural intelligence is the capability to interact effectively with people from different cultural backgrounds' (Thomas and Inkson, 2003, p.62).

With the increase of cross-cultural interactions and transactions, the market for cross-cultural training increases as well and many courses and books are concentrating on effective cross-cultural managing. Hofstede's (1980) cultural dimensions are used widely as a basis of understanding one's own culture and the host culture (French, 2010). MNCs are hiring cultural experts to train their employees specifically for their operations in the host country. Hofstede's (2009a) work represents the 'edge of understanding' of culture and helps managers to be aware of cultural differences. The explicit cultural dimension scores make the cultural difference feasible and visible, hence managers can be trained to handle and manage these differences effectively (Thomas and Inkson, 2003). Moreover, Bing (2004) lists several examples of practical applications in which context the cultural dimension of Hofstede are being used:

TABLE IX:

EXAMPLES OF PRACTICAL APPLICATIONS OF HOFSTEDE'S WORK

Orientation and Training	Leadership Training and Development	Business Practices
new employee orientation	models of leadership	managing cross-border mergers and acquisitions
multicultural workplaces	management practices	leveraging joint ventures
relocation training	communicating across geographic and institutional boundaries	vetting employee surveys
developing nuanced global business practices	global teams	negotiations
	development of global competencies	content-specific business practices
		globalizing functions
		the impact of culture on change strategy

(Source: Bing, 2004, p.82)

The cultural dimensions scores can explain different approaches of working behaviour and makes it easier to understand and to handle cultural misunderstandings. For example, employees in high PD cultures tend to copy their immediate supervisors on most emails, which is often misunderstood by low PD colleagues (Bing, 2004).

Hofstede's (2001) cultural dimensions make it possible to train and teach managers especially for international business relations in a specific country.

Furthermore, Hofstede and his son wrote the book '*The Ten Synthetic Cultures*' about training methods and simulations in which they demonstrate the impact of national culture to practical use. This book is specifically aimed to cross-cultural managers and to help and support them in international business relations (Hofstede *et al.*, 2002). For each dimensions the extreme poles are explained and typical behaviour and characteristics are discussed. For example, employees in individualistic cultures hold according to Hofstede *et al.* (2002, p. 94) seven key elements:

TABLE X:

KEY ELEMENTS OF EMPLOYEES IN INDIVIDUALISTIC CULTURES

1. Honest people speak their mind.
2. Low-context communication (explicit concepts) is preferred.
3. The task takes precedence over relationships.
4. Laws and rights are the same for all.
5. Trespassing leads to guilt and loss of self-respect.
6. Everyone is supposed to have a personal opinion on any topic.
7. The relationship between employer and employee or between parent and child is a contract based on mutual advantage.

(Source: Hofstede *et al.*, 2002, p. 94)

The whole book explains several practical tips and hints for the usage of each dimension and helps managers to understand and manage cultural differences. Hofstede *et al.* (2002) offer a theoretical basis for a practical use; however, it is hard to say in absolute terms to what extent Hofstede (1980) actually adds value to managers' daily life.

Further, Harvey (1997, p.144) suggests that 'Hofstede's dimensions of national culture are a good basis for understanding the influence of national culture on organizations' self representation', and is therefore widely used within training and workshops.

CHAPTER 3

3 RESEARCH METHODOLOGY

Research methodology is seen as the 'theory of how research should be undertaken including the theoretical and philosophical assumptions upon which research is based and the implications of these for the method or methods adopted' (Saunders *et al.*, 2009, p.595). In this chapter the research process is explained and justified, data validity and reliability is ensured, research ethics are considered and limitations are assessed.

3.1 RESEARCH PROCESS

According to Saunders *et al.* (2009) the research process can be symbolised as an onion. Several layers of the onion need to be peeled away before reaching the central point and core of the onion, the data collection and data analysis. Figure 4 shows the research onion and the structure of this chapter. The outer layer, philosophies and approaches and the middle layers of strategies, choices and time horizon are guarding the way towards the core of the onion and the research methodology: the techniques and procedures. Highlighted are the strategies and approaches that are used within this study, which are explained in more detail below.

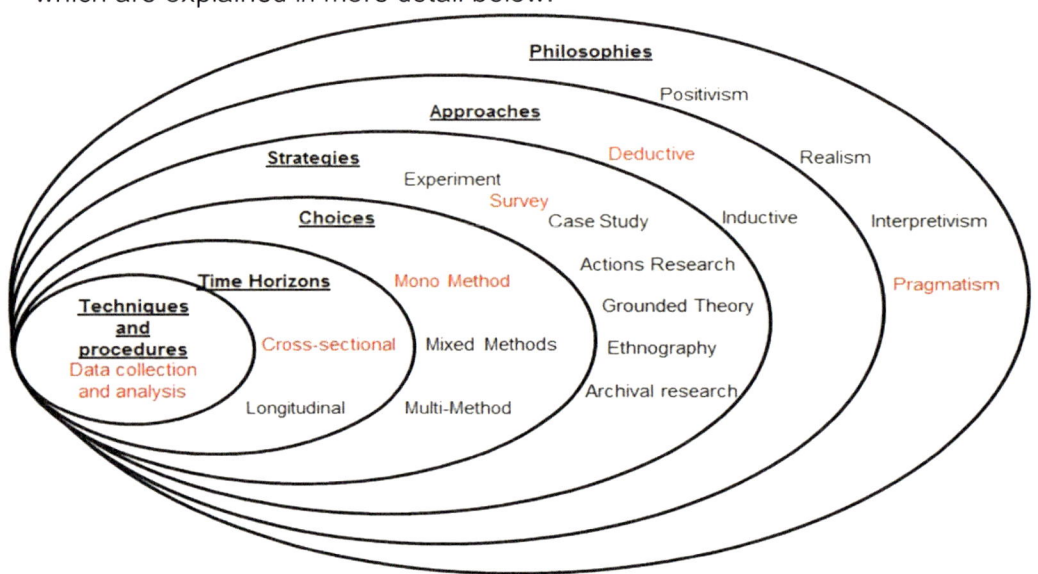

FIGURE 4: THE RESEARCH ONION (Source: Saunders *et al.*, 2009, p. 108)

3.1.1 Philosophy of research

A philosophical framework guides the way scientific research is conducted and is influenced by people's idea of the reality which changes over time (Collis and Hussey, 2009). This results in the emergence of new research paradigm, which are described by Kuhn (1962, p.viii) as 'universally recognized scientific achievements that for a time provide model problems and solution to a community of practitioners'.

Research philosophy 'relates to the development of knowledge and the nature of that knowledge' (Saunders *et al.*, 2009, p.128). Epistemology, Ontology and Axiology are three ways of thinking about research philosophy and the main research philosophies are Positivism, Interpretivism, Realism and Pragmatism. The latter argues that the most important determinant is the research question and the possibility to work within Positivism and Interpretivism is given, as this practical approach includes various perspectives to support gathering data and interpreting those (Saunders *et al.*, 2009). Positivism is originated in the natural sciences and stresses the belief that social reality is singular and objective and not affected by the investigation of it. Underpinned by precision, objectivity and rigour, causal relationships are analysed with the help of explanatory theories to understand social phenomena (Collis and Hussey, 2009). Resulting from criticisms of Positivism, Interpretivism emerged, as it concentrates on exploring social complexity with the purpose to gain interpretive understanding, while Positivism is only focusing on measuring and explaining social phenomena (Collis and Hussey, 2009). Furthermore, Gill and Johnson (2010) state that the process of investigating affects the social reality and is subjective as well as multiple.

A Subjectivism ontological way of thinking about research philosophy is influencing the research process of this study, as the study tries to explore and understand the subjective meanings of actions and behaviour of German and British students. Further, this study's research philosophy reflects the stance of Pragmatism. The research question is the most important determinant in this study and dependant on the type of question one approach might be better than another (Von der Gracht, 2008). Therefore, both philosophies of Positivism and Interpretivism are adapted:

- *To what extent are Hofstede's findings reliable, valid and applicable to organisations in the 21st century?*

The research question is based on existing theory and studies and is critically evaluating the literature. Further to investigate in how far Hofstede's model has not changed over time, hypotheses are defined. These hypotheses are tested and evaluated within the framework of Positivism as a deductive approach. First, through measuring the phenomena, an interpretive understanding is developed, which indicates an Interpretivism philosophy (Collis and Hussey, 2009). While many authors outline Positivism and Interpretivism as mutual exclusive and extremes, Saunders *et al.* (2009) and Collis and Hussey (2009) combine these philosophies into the Pragmatism, which offers this study a balance of both philosophies; and the weaknesses of one philosophy can be offset with the strengths of the other

3.1.2 Research Approach

The research approach is subdivided into two research types of reasoning: the deductive and inductive approach (Gill and Johnson, 2009). Within the deductive approach a theory and hypotheses are developed and a strategy is designed to test the Hypotheses (Saunders *et al.*, 2009). Figure 5 illustrates the 'top-down' approach which works from general and broad information, to specific reasoning.

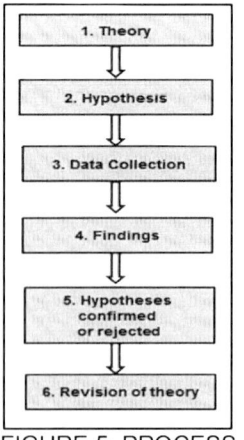

FIGURE 5: PROCESS OF DEDUCTION
(Source: Bryman and Bell, 2003, p.11)

Bryman and Bell (2003, p.11) outline that 'theory and the hypothesis deduced from it come first and drive the process of gathering data'. By analysing the data the hypotheses are either confirmed or rejected and the theory is revised again (Bryman and Bell, 2003).

The inductive approach is the contrary, as the first step is the data collection and a theory is developed after the analysis of that data (Saunders *et al.*, 2009). This approach is referred to as moving from the specific to the general and 'theory is developed from the observation of empirical reality thus general inferences are induced from particular instances' (Collis and Hussey, 2009, p.8).

The research question is partly Positivism as mentioned above, which is according to Saunders *et al.* (2009) useful to attach deduction. The analysis of the reliability, validity and application of Hofstede's (1980) model are following a deductive approach, as Hypotheses are formulated:

H_1: The cultural dimension of Masculinity/ Femininity has not changed over time and Germany and UK are still very masculine countries with similar scores (66).

H_2: The cultural dimension of Uncertainty Avoidance has not changed over time and Germany still scores higher (65) than the UK (35).

These hypotheses are driving the process of gathering data and the research strategy. As according to Ghauri and Grønhaug (2010, p.15) 'this type of research [...] deduces hypotheses from the existing knowledge (literature), which can be subject to empirical scrutiny (testing) and thus can be accepted or rejected'. Hofstede's (1980) dimensions are criticised to be old-fashioned and not contemporary anymore. Deduce from this knowledge the hypotheses are formulated to proof within an empirical research and collection of quantitative data, if they have to be accepted or rejected (Ghauri and Grønhaug, 2010; Saunders *et al.*, 2009).

3.1.3 Research Strategy

After peeling off the outer layers of the research onion, the focus lies on the research design, which is framed by the previous choices of philosophies and approaches (Saunders *et al.*, 2009). Furthermore, the research design creates a framework and a plan for the core of the onion - the data collection and its analysis (Ghauri and Grønhaug, 2010).

There are several different research strategies which can be selected, like experiment, survey, case study, action research, grounded theory, ethnography and archival research. The choice of strategy is guided by the research question and the objectives and several resources as existing knowledge or time (Saunders *et al.*, 2009). As the research question is considering the validation, reliability and applicable approach of Hofstede's (1980) findings, a survey was chosen to evaluate to what extent the dimensions still exists using the example of Germany and the UK. Formulating the hypotheses, the survey strategy is associated with the deductive approach and positivist philosophy (Collis and Hussey, 2009). 'Surveys attempt to gather information from an entire group, or more usually a sample, which can be used to make inferences or generate policy or reveal unsuspected facts' (Swetman and Swetman, 2009, p.33). Surveys and especially questionnaires are the most popular data collection methods in business studies and have several advantages as well as disadvantages, which is shown in Table XI (Ghauri and Grønhaug, 2010).

TABLE XI:

ADVANTAGES AND DISADVANTAGES OF QUESTIONNAIRES

Advantages	Disadvantages
Money saving	Narrow sample
Time saving	Inability to ask questions in return
Anonymity	Possibility of a biased sample
Ease of completion	
Remote location	

(Source: Bailey, 1994, pp.204-207)

3.1.4 Research Choices

The research choice is the way in which the combination of qualitative and quantitative techniques and procedures are chosen (Saunders *et al.*, 2009). Qualitative research is a descriptive form of research that is 'covering an array of interpretative techniques which seek to describe, decode, translate, and otherwise come to term with the meaning of naturally occurring phenomena in the social world' (Kruger *et al.*, 2005, p.188). On the other hand, quantitative data is in a numerical form and express in the form of numbers, information about the world or the analysed topic (Punch, 2005). A choice of a data collection technique, like the mono, multi or mixed method, has to be made before the actual collection. The mono method is considering single data collection techniques and corresponding analysis procedures, while the multiple-method is using more than one technique and analysis procedures and is further subdivided into multi- and mixed- methods (Saunders *et al.*, 2009).

According to McNeil and Chapman (2005) the Positivism approach is likely to be attached to the deductive approach through questionnaires to produce quantitative data. This study is considering quantitative data through conducting questionnaires in Germany and the UK and is therefore choosing a mono-method.

3.1.5 Time Horizon

The time horizon of a research process is dependent on the research question and the strategies and can be divided into a cross-sectional and longitudinal study. The cross-sectional study is a 'study of a particular phenomenon at a particular time' (Saunders *et al.*, 2009, p.155), while the longitudinal is a study over a longer period of time. Considering the time limit, this study is undertaking a cross-sectional study. As Hofstede started his analysis of the cultural dimension with a cross-sectional study as well in 1968 and later conducted another study in 1972, the snapshot of this specific time in 2010 can be compared to the snapshots in 1968 and 1972.

3.1.6 Data collection method

There are several sources of information that can be used for research. The two main types of data collection are primary and secondary data, which are both used within this study. Onkvisit and Shaw (2004) state, that the advantages of primary research are the disadvantages of secondary and vice versa. Therefore a study should start by considering secondary research and apply primary research where needed in order to prove or reject findings from the secondary data or to add further value to already existing data.

Secondary Research: The collection and evaluation of secondary data was necessary to analyse the current state of the knowledge in the subject area of culture, cross-cultural management, globalisation and specifically in Hofstede's (1980) cultural dimensions. Furthermore, the wider context of the subject needed to be known, as well as the limitations and opportunities. Secondary data 'are data collected from an existing source (for example publications, databases and internal records)' (Collis and Hussey, 2009, p.23) and need to be studied before further research is done. In this study, the several editions of Hofstede's books (1980; 1991; 1996; 2001; 2004; 2010) and his articles constituted a theoretical framework for further researches and analysis. Related articles, books and criticism of Hofstede's (1980) findings resulted in the critical literature review (Chapter 2) which includes earlier studies and research on and around this topic (Ghauri and Grønhaug, 2010). An inductive approach of analysing secondary data was used, as secondary data was collected and analysed to be able to develop theoretical reasoning.

Secondary data has got several advantages and disadvantages which need to be considered. These are shown in Table XII below:

TABLE XII:

ADVANTAGES AND DISADVANTAGES OF SECONDARY DATA

Advantages of Secondary data	**Disadvantages of Secondary data**
Time and money saving	Might be biased
Broad amount of data	Out-of-date
Different perspectives and opinions	Might be unreliable
Most data is high quality and reliable	A poor 'fit'
Comparison element	No control over data collection
Availability	
Flexibility	

(Source: Ghauri and Grønhaug, 2010, pp.94-96; Loudon *et al.*, 2007, pp.72/73; Saunders *et al.*, 2009, pp.288-272; Schmidt and Hollensen, 2006, p.16)

Secondary data within this study is carefully analysed and reviewed, as it might be biased, out of date and not reliable, but it is time and money saving, offer a broad amount of data, several perspectives and opinions and a lot of data is of high quality and reliable.

Saunders *et al.* (2009) explain several different types of secondary data, such as documentary, multiple source and survey secondary data. The multiple source and survey secondary data is used within this study, as especially Hofstede's (1980) survey and study of cultural dimensions is analysed and evaluated. Furthermore, the secondary research about Hofstede's (1980) survey and especially the criticism of the questionnaire framed and structured the primary research, which is further discussed.

Primary Research: Primary data is 'collected from an original source' (Collis and Hussey, 2009, p.23) and for a specific purpose (Kruger *et al.*, 2005). Conducting primary data is very time consuming and highly dependent on the sample and response rate, but it is tailored to the research need, hence very contemporary. Further advantages and disadvantages are assembled in Table XIII.

TABLE XIII:

ADVANTAGES AND DISADVANTAGES OF PRIMARY DATA

Advantages of Primary data	Disadvantages of Primary data
Tailored to research needs	Time and money consuming
Based on study-specific tools	Dependant on response rate
Contemporary	Low accessibility
	Low Flexibility
	Risk of low reliability
	Risk of losing control

(Source: Ghauri and Grønhaug, 2010, pp.99/100)

The secondary research undertaken in the literature review discovered a need for further primary research to evaluate the validity, applicability and out-dated findings of Hofstede (1980). As this study is using questionnaires as a primary research technique, the most important parts of conducting primary data within questionnaires, is the questionnaire itself and its sample.

Sampling: 'A sample is a subset of a population' (Collis and Hussey, 2009, p.76) and is widely used within positivist studies as a representative sample size allows researchers to generalize their findings. As it is mostly impossible to collect data from a whole population due to time, money and access limitations, several sample techniques enable a generalisation from sub-groups to the broader public (Saunders *et al.*, 2009). Sampling can be divided into two main techniques: probability and non-probability sample, which can be further sub-divided into several concrete techniques (Kruger *et al.*, 2005). A probability sample contains the equal probability that any element or member of the population could be included in the sample, whereas in a non-probability sample elements and members of a population have not an equal chance of being included in the sample (Collis and Hussey, 2009). This study operates with a basis of non-probability and purpose sampling.

However, Collis and Hussey (2009) argue that a non-probability sample is not representative for a whole population as it has certain limits and causes risk for errors of estimation. Due to the fact that the analysis of cultural differences needs to match on certain criteria to filter the cultural differences, a probability sample is not suitable in this specific case.

Hofstede *et al.* (2008a, p.3) state in the Value Survey Module 2008 Manual, that 'comparisons of countries should be based on samples of respondents who are matched on all criteria other than nationality that could systematically affect the answers'. Furthermore, the Chinese Value Survey, which Hofstede used for his 5th dimension of Long-term orientation, was answered by 100 students in 23 countries (Hofstede *et al.*, 2010). This study, led by Michael Bond, was only considering students, as 'the additional dimension was found in a comparison of students in 23 countries' (Hofstede *et al.*, 2008a, p.2). Thus, students in Germany and the UK were considered to be the best possible sampling, due to comparison reasons as well as access possibilities. Therefore, to analyse the cultural differences between Germany and UK within the two cultural dimensions (MAS/ UA) the samples of both countries needed to 'match on all criteria other than nationality' (Hofstede *et al.*, 2008a, p.3). The undergraduate module of 'Entrepreneurial Business Innovation', which is taught in the third year at the Oxford Brookes University in Oxford, UK and the 'Basics principles of business studies' (Grundlagen der BWL), which is taught in the first year at the University of Applied Science Fresenius (Hochschule Fresenius) in Cologne, Germany are presenting matching conditions and criteria where only the nationality differs. Due to the fact that undergraduate students start studying at universities one year earlier, due to different durations of high school in the countries, the age average of 20,7 for Germany and 21,2 for UK is considered relatively the same.

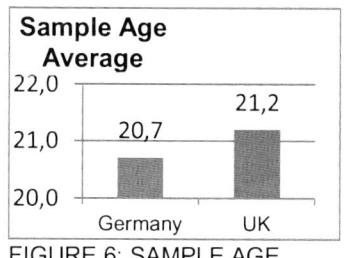

FIGURE 6: SAMPLE AGE AVERAGE (Source: Own illustration)

Moreover, both modules are thought in relation to business, which secures the similarity of the study area and hence a comparable background (Fresenius, 2010; Oxford Brookes University, 2010).

Considering the sample size, Ghauri and Grønhaug (2010, p.144) state the sample size 'depends on the desired precision from the estimate'. Hofstede *et al.* (2008a; 2009b) suggest that 50 respondents are an ideal size for a homogenous sample and due to the fact that within the Chinese Value Survey a minimum of 100 students was conducted, this study complies with a sample size of a minimum of 100 students as well.

Resulting, 147 undergraduate students from the 'Entrepreneurial Business Innovation' module at the Oxford Brookes University (OBU) in Oxford, UK and 110 undergraduate student from the 'Basics principles of business studies' module (Grundlagen der BWL) at the University of Applied Science Fresenius (Hochschule Fresenius/ HF) in Cologne, Germany were surveyed in this primary research. With a response rate of 100%, where 63% (104) were valid British questionnaires (43 International Students = 37%) and 95,6% (106) valid German questionnaires (4 International Students = 4,4%), a total of 257 questionnaires was obtained (of which 210 are considered valid).

The concrete survey sample is illustrated in Figure 7:

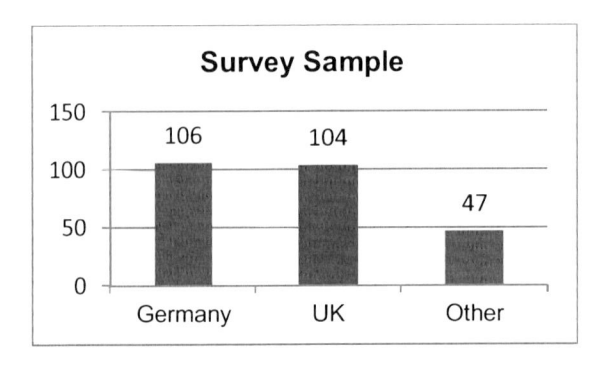

FIGURE 7: SURVEY SAMPLE (Source: Own illustration)

Questionnaire design and distribution: A questionnaire can be distributed in several different ways, and Saunders *et al.* (2009) distinguish between self-administered and interviewer-administered, as shown in Figure 8 below.

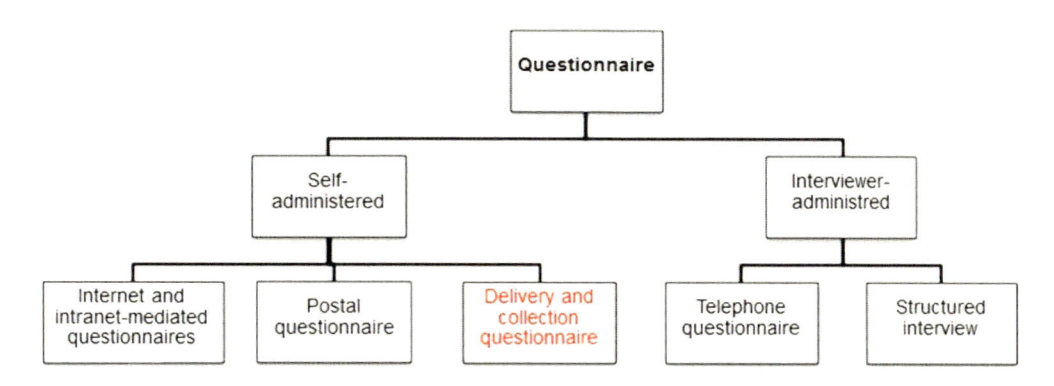

FIGURE 8: TYPES OF QUESTIONNAIRES (Source: Saunders *et al.*, 2009, p.363)

The choice of questionnaire affects the response rate and is affected by several personal resources such as time, money and access (Saunders *et al.*, 2009). This study undertook a self-administered delivery and collection questionnaire, as the questionnaires were delivered by hand to the respondents and collected later. With this type of questionnaire distribution it is possible to ensure that the right people answered the questions and respondents are unlikely to answer the questions to please the researcher, as the direct contact to the researcher is limited and anonymity is given (Dillman, 2007). Furthermore, Saunders *et al.* (2009) state, that a high response rate is possible due to direct influence and personal initiative, which explains the 100% response rate of this self-administered questionnaire which was used within the presented study.

Furthermore, several attributes of the delivery and collection questionnaires that were used within this study are discussed in Table XIV below:

TABLE XIV:

MAIN ATTRIBUTES OF SELF-ADMINISTERED DELIVERY AND COLLECTION QUESTIONNAIRES

Attribute	Delivery and collection
Population's characteristics	Undergraduate students from Oxford Brookes University in Oxford, UK and Undergraduate students from University of applied Science, Fresenius, Cologne, Germany. OBU: Entrepreneurial Business Innovation module (3rd year) HF: 'Grundlagen der BWL' (Basics principles of business studies) (1st year)
Confidence that right person has responded	In general *low, but can be checked at collection*; However- in this study high, because distribution undertaken directly in the courses
Likelihood of contamination of respondent's answer	May be contaminated by consultation with others
Size of sample	OBU: 147 (valid: 104) HF: 110 (valid: 106) Others: 47
Response rate	100%
Feasible length of questionnaire	3 A4 pages (2 pages on 1 sheet; double paged) + 1 Information Sheet
Suitable types of question	Closed questions but not too complex, simple sequencing only, must be of interest to respondent
Time taken to complete collection	→ 1 day in Oxford (Thursday, 25th November) → 2 days in Cologne (Tuesday, 30th November and Wednesday, 1st December)
Main financial resource implications	Travel to Germany and back(£148); Photocopying (£50)
Role of the interviewer/ field worker	Delivery and collections of questionnaires, enhancing respondent participation
Data input	Closed questions can be designed so that responses may be entered using optical mark readers after questionnaire has been returned

(Source: Own illustration based on Saunders *et al.*, 2009, p.364)

The questionnaire design affects the internal validity and reliability of the collected data, as well as the response rate (Saunders *et al.*, 2009). Thus, each question has to be carefully considered and assessed. Three different approaches for posing questions are discussed by Saunders *et al.* (2009): Adopting questions; adapting questions or developing own questions. As this study's aim is to compare findings with Hofstede's (2001), some questions from the VSM 08 are adopted and adapted. The validity of Hofstede's (2008b) questionnaire was criticised, as he did not intend to analyse the cultural dimension and the questions were not posed for this specific purpose. Further the statistical integrity was questionable, as Hofstede (2008a) used the same questionnaire item on more than one scale and several items had significant cross-loadings, like 32 questions with 40 cases or subjects (Dorfman and Howell, 1988). Such an 'analysis built on so few subjects takes great advantage of chance and increases the likelihood of sample errors' (Dorfman and Howell, 1988).

Resulting from these criticisms, the questionnaire that was used within this study adopted the Questions 1, 3 and 10 from the VSM08 questionnaire (Hofstede *et al.*, 2008a), whereas the other questions were adapted and varied from Hofstede's 'Culture Consequences' (2001) book and the European Value Survey (Inglehart, 2000). Hofstede's VSM08 (Hofstede *et al.*, 2008a; 2008b) questions are not under copyright and can be freely used for research purpose as he explains on the cover letter of the VSM08 (Hofstede *et al.*, 2008b). Hofstede *et al.* (2008a) released a VSM08 Manual to explain the way cultural dimension scores are calculated and where specific questions are the indicator for the dimensions. Due to time and word limit within this research process, this thesis has a focus on two dimensions to enable an in-depth and detailed analysis. Germany and UK score similar on the Masculinity/ Femininity (MAS) index in Hofstede's IBM study with 66. Whereas, the Uncertainty Avoidance (UA) index demonstrates a big gap between Germany and UK, as Germany scores relatively high with 65 and UK relatively low with 35 (Hofstede *et al.*, 2010). The Masculinity/ Femininity dimension was chosen due to the similarity in scores, while Uncertainty Avoidance was chosen, because of the big difference. Therefore, a balance is given between one equal and one unequal dimension, which make the analysis more interesting and profound. Hofstede *et al.* (2008a) sets in his VSM08 Manuel index formulas for each dimension, which determined the questions chosen in the questionnaire. The calculation of the indices is further discussed in Chapter 4.

The questionnaire uses only closed questions, as due to the quantity of responses it is faster and easier to analyse, evaluate and compare. Moreover the time to answer the questionnaire is reduced, which further increases the response rate (Collis and Hussey, 2009). Several types of closed questions are used within this study: List questions, Category questions, Ranking and Rating Questions. Moreover, the Likert-style rating scale is used for the indicator questions to calculate the mean scores out of a five-point rating scale (Saunders *et al.*, 2009). While posing the questions, it is important to consider how the analysis of the research data is going to be done. Therefore pre-coding questions for statistical analysis makes the final analysis easier and more convenient (Collis and Hussey, 2009). The questionnaire, which was used within this study, was pre-coded like Hofstede's questionnaire with a 5 point Likert scale (Hofstede, 2001).

Moreover, the questionnaire was distributed in German and English and originally adopted from Hofstede's *et al.* (2008b) German and English VSM08 questionnaire version and from the English and German book edition. Especially for international research, it is important that the questions have the same meaning to all respondents (Saunders *et al.*, 2009). Due to the fact that the questions were adopted from a German and English Version of the VSM08 questionnaire and the national language editions, the concerns about translation errors is low. In addition, the two language versions were proofed by several bi-lingual Germans to secure a high probability of correct translation. At last, the final questionnaire was pilot tested with ten German speaking and ten English speaking students, in order to give some information about reliability and validity.

Swetman and Swetman (2009) state several points that need to be considered while posing questions, such as using simple, direct and appropriate language, simple multiple choices questions where 'don't' know', 'none of these' or 'other' category is given. Further, they argue that a questionnaire always needs to be headed and explained. Therefore, an information sheet was added, where the overall purpose and brief details are outlined (Appendix B). The two questionnaires are shown in Appendix C and Appendix D.

3.2 DATA VALIDITY, RELIABILITY AND GENERALISIBILITY

'A valid questionnaire will enable accurate data to be collected, and one that is reliable will mean that these data are collected consistently' (Saunders *et al.*, 2009, p.371). Furthermore, validity and reliability ensure that the questions and answers are making sense. Foddy (1994) introduces four stages which must take place if the reliability and validity of a question should be secured. Figure 9 demonstrates the four stages:

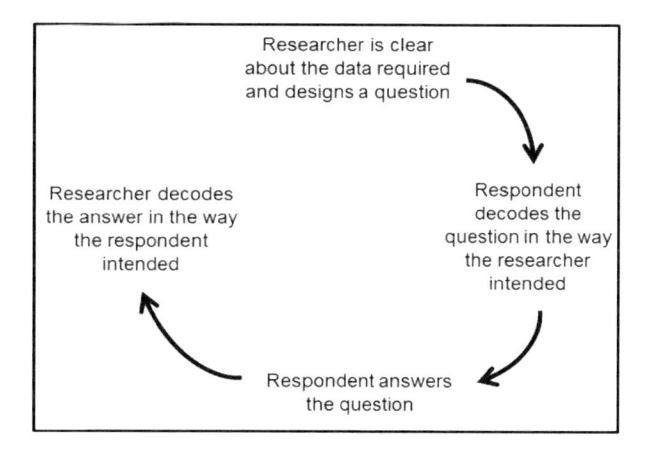

FIGURE 9: STAGES THAT MUST OCCUR IF A QUESTION IS TO BE VALID AND RELIABLE
(Source: Foddy (1994) in Saunders *et al.*, 2009, p. 372)

3.2.1 Validity

Validity is 'an indication of accuracy in terms of the extent to which a research conclusion corresponds with reality' (McBurney and White, 2010, p.173) and Collis and Hussey (2009) add, that validity indicates the representation of a true picture of what has been studied. Further, McNeil and Chapman (2005) outline the danger, that a survey can only collect people's answers to questions, which might not present a true picture of their activities. Validity can be distinguished between internal and external validity, where the internal validity is describes as the 'ability [...] to measure what you intend to measure' (Saunders *et al.*, 2009, p.372). This study adopted the questions from the VSM08 (Hofstede *et al.*, 2008b), Hofstede's 2001 edition and the European Value Survey (Inglehart, 2000) and assumed that these conducted questionnaires were the results of long experienced researchers who are well known in their field of study and are well aware of the internal validity. One question was exchanged, due to its doubts about its validity, which in return should further increase the questionnaire overall validity.

The external validity on the other side is explained by McBurney and White (2010, p.176) as in how far 'the results of the research can be generalized to another situation'. With a sample size of 275, with 110 in Germany and 147 in the UK, the threat of the external validity can be decreased, as the bigger the sample size the smaller the threat of external validity (Kruger *et al.*, 2005).

The collection of secondary data was handled with the same caution as the collection of the primary data. As Saunders *et al.* (2009) stress the importance of evaluating and critically assessing secondary data sources, the data sources which related to the research aim and objectives were critically analysed and handled with concerns. Further, the sources were evaluated and additional research was made to secure the quality of the sources and increase the validity. Irrelevant data was excluded, as Ghauri and Grønhaug (2010) suggests that from the huge amount of secondary data available, data needs to be extracted and critical judgement needs to be applied to concentrate on the essential data relevant for the research question. Moreover, the context and process in which the data was collected were examined, whenever possible. As Dochartaigh (2002) suggests an assessment of the authority of documents via the internet, this study critically assessed these. Likewise, internet sources were handled with caution and care, as publications might not have been controlled and the probability of non-quality papers is higher due to the huge amount of data available on the internet (Ghauri and Grønhaug, 2010). Browne (2005) continues this discussion, as inaccurate and unreliable information indicates a lack of validity, which further might be biased, contains errors or be exaggerated. Therefore, a focus was made on copyright statements and the existence of published documents relating to the data in order to support validation. The question for the responsibility of the data is provided by the copyright statement, whereas published documents reinforce the data's authority, as they are regarded to be more reliable (Saunders *et al.*, 2009). To understand different phenomena and to enhance the validity of this study, various findings were triangulated to carry out cross-check verifications (Patzer, 1996).

3.2.2 Reliability

Reliability refers to particular research techniques and methods and 'the extent to which they yield a consistent result when used on more than one occasion or by different people' (Bulmer, 1984, p.30). Moreover, reliability refers to consistency and is concerned with the robustness of the questionnaire and whether consistent findings under different conditions and factors can be made (Saunders *et al.*, 2009). Cohen *et al.* (2007) distinguish the term reliability between qualitative and quantitative research. Regarding quantitative research, which is used within this study, reliability refers to 'dependability, consistency and replicability over time, over instruments and over groups of respondents' (Cohen *et al.*, 2007, p.146). However, Robson

(2002) argues that if a questionnaire is not reliable, it cannot be valid. But as reliability is necessary, it does not ensure validity.

The majority of primary data is collected via questionnaires and its validity and reliability can be better ensured through pilot testing. This enhances the validity of the questionnaire by collecting accurate data and the reliability of consistent findings (Saunders *et al.*, 2009). The pilot testing of ten German and ten British students attempts to ensure the reliability. Moreover, the reliability can be assessed with three approaches: the test re-test, the internal consistency and the alternative form. Due to time limitations a test re-test was not possible, but applying internal consistency and the alternative form can secure the questionnaires reliability. The internal consistency measures the consistency of responses, where several questions are correlated within the questionnaire. This will be further discussed in Chapter 4. 'Check questions' are used within the alternative form in the questionnaire to compare alternative forms of the same questions and to analyse its consistency (Saunders *et al.*, 2009). Moreover, Robson (2002) argues that there are several threats to reliability: subject or participant error, subject or participant bias, observer error or observer bias. To overcome these threats, firstly the question which was identified as a subject or participant error (Question m20) was exchanged, which is further described in Chapter 4.2. Moreover, the primary research was conducted by a single person and the questionnaires were answered anonymously to lessen the threats of unreliability.

As mentioned before, secondary data is the main source of written studies and need to be critically assessed of its quality and reliability (Ghauri and Grønhaug, 2010). Secondary data has some disadvantages such as selectivity, limited accessibility and reporting bias (Schlevogt, 2002). Thus, the information research of secondary data was obtained carefully and several sources such as books, scholarly, peer-reviewed journals and quality webpages were considered. However, Anderson (2004) argues that there is no actual control over written secondary data and studies cannot be fully reliable and valid.

3.2.3 Generalisability

Generalisability is defined as the 'extent to which the findings of a research study are applicable to other settings' (Saunders *et al.*, 2009, p. 592) and can be referred to 'external validity', which was mentioned before already. With a sample size of 257 respondents and 104 valid British and 106 valid German responses, the generalisability might be limited due to its non-probability sample origin and a relative small sample compared to the whole population (Collis and Hussey, 2009; Kruger *et al.*, 2005). Even though, Hofstede *et al.* (2008a) state, that a minimum of 50 respondents is required, a comparison with Hofstede's (2001) German (7,907) and British (3,731) respondents shows the relative limitation of the sample size.

3.3 RESEARCH ETHICS

Research ethics is 'the appropriateness of the researcher's behaviour in relation to the rights of those who become the subject of a research project, or who are affected by it' (Saunders *et al.*, 2009, p.600). As researchers have a moral responsibility in the way of explaining and finding answers to their questions honestly and accurately, ethical issues have to be addressed and considered (Ghauri and Grønhaug, 2010). The main ethical issues that are discussed in the literature are anonymity and confidentiality, voluntary nature, informed consent, protected from any harm, legality and morality, and privacy (Ghauri and Grønhaug, 2010; Saunders *et al.*, 2009; Collis and Hussey, 2009; McNeil and Chapman, 2005; Kruger *et al.*, 2005). Collis and Hussey (2009) further state, that organisations, companies, associations and universities often have their own ethic policies which need to be considered and observed. Therefore, the Universities Code of Practice of 'Ethical standards for research involving human participants' (Oxford Brookes University, 2000), which is shown in Appendix E, was strictly adhered throughout the whole research process. The main principles and especially the 'ethical imperatives of DO NO HARM (nonmaleficience) and DO GOOD (beneficience)' (Oxford Brookes University, 2000, p.1) were considered.

3.4 LIMITATIONS

'A limitation is a weakness or deficiency in the research' (Collis and Hussey, 2009, p.125). Several limitations are constraining this study and need to be addressed at this point. The critique of Hofstede's (2001) survey might apply to this study as well, as it is argued by some researchers, that a questionnaire is not an appropriate tool to study culture. However, as this survey is a replication, there is no alternative. Furthermore, Hofstede (2010) himself argues in general, that given answers might not always represent the actual behaviour of a respondent. This could endanger the validity and as McNeil and Chapman (2005) state, not present the true picture. A crucial limitation is the sample size and the location of conducting the primary data. 275 students at only two universities might not be a representative sample, even though Hofstede *et al.* (2008a) claims that 50 respondents is an ideal size. But due to time and money limitations a larger sample size was not operable. A further criticism might be that the university's internal culture might have affected the student's behaviour. As researchers claim that organisational culture influences employee's behaviour, universities culture might have an influence on student's behaviour. Gooderham and Nordhaug (2001) criticised Hofstede of being culturally biased, which might apply to this study as well. The cultural background of the researcher of this study might have an influence of this study, as the home country is compared with the current country of residence.

While analysing the survey, another limitation appeared within Question 9. This Check Question asks the participants to rank the most important factors in an ideal job from 1-3. This question was misunderstood by 20% of all the participants, as participants tended to tick all factors except of just three. Therefore it creates a limitation due to its invalid answers. However, 10% were categorised to 'Other Countries' and therefore only the other 10% affects the result.

Furthermore, reasons for a difference of the scores are hard to define and only suggestions could be made, which creates a lack of proof in the presented explanations. Many external factors could influence the study and its result, like point in time, current economic situations, current labour market, *etc.* but it is not clear to what extent which factor is really affecting the findings.

CHAPTER 4

4 ANALYSIS AND FINDINGS

In this chapter the findings of the primary survey are going to be analysed and the validity, reliability and contemporary aspect of Hofstede's (1980) study are evaluated. Furthermore, personal dimension scores are calculated according to Hofstede's *et al.* (2008a) approach. The approach and the findings are discussed and the Hypotheses are assessed.

4.1 INTRODUCTION

This study includes a small replication study of Hofstede's (1980) IBM study, where two countries are analysed within two dimensions. Thus, as explained before, individual scores for Masculinity (MAS) and Uncertainty Avoidance (UA) are calculated for Germany and the UK. These indices and further results of the survey are analysed and discussed in the following section. To conclude the findings are discussed and the Hypotheses are evaluated:

- H_1: The cultural dimension of Masculinity/ Femininity has not changed over time and Germany and UK are still very masculine countries with similar scores (66).

- H_2: The cultural dimension of Uncertainty Avoidance has not changed over time and Germany still scores higher (65) than the UK (35).

The data analysis started after the first conducted primary research on Thursday, 25th of November 2010 at the Oxford Brookes University in Oxford UK. The process of analysis was done manually, supported by Microsoft Excel 2010 and resulted in the data sheet, which is shown in Appendix F. Moreover, output-charts were created for each question to analyse directly and convenient the differences between Germany and the UK, as shown in Appendix G.

4.2 CALCULATION OF DIMENSION SCORES

This study tries to analyse the present similarities and differences of Germany and UK within the cultural dimension of MAS and UA and will calculate own cultural scores based on the primary data collected. These scores cannot be directly compared with Hofstede's (2001) scores, as Hofstede *et al.* (2008a, p.5) explains 'that comparisons of countries should be based on matched samples of respondents: people who are similar on all criteria other than nationality that could systematically affect the answers'. Further, he criticised 'enthusiastic amateurs' (Hofstede *et al.*, 2008a, p.5) using a sample of respondents from a single country and trying to compare them with the scores of the IBM study. Thus, this study can calculate its own dimension scores for Germany and UK based on the data provided by a matching sample of students, and can only analyse and evaluate the relative differences and tendencies of these scores with Hofstede's (1980) originally scores. However, this study will not be able to directly compare its own scores with Hofstede's (1980).

As described in Chapter 3.1.6, Hofstede *et al.* (2008a) composed a VSM08 Manual to calculate the dimension scores which were used within this study to calculate individual MAS and UA scores for Germany and the UK.

The index formula for MAS is the following:

$$MAS = 35(m05 - m03) + 35(m08 - m10) + C(mf) \qquad (1)$$

In which m05 is the mean score of Question 5, *etc.* in the VSM questionnaire. 35 represents the weighting factor of the equations and C(mf) is a constant (positive or negative) which is dependent on the nature of the sample, but is not affecting the comparison of countries. As the index has normally a range between 0 and 100 (strongly feminine and strongly masculine) the constant can be individually chosen to range the scores between 0 and 100. The questions m05 and m08 indicate feminine attributes as m05 is asking for the evaluation of how important cooperation with colleagues is and m08 evaluates the importance of the living area. Thus, m05 and m08 are the minuend of the difference and feminine attributes, whereas m03 and m10 are the subtrahend, and masculine indicating attributes. The question m03 asks for the importance of recognition and m10 for the importance of advancement.

Adopting the index formula to the questionnaires used in this study creates the following MAS formula:

$$MAS = 35(m10f - m10b) + 35(m10g - m10c) + C(mf) \qquad (2)$$

Therefore, the indicator questions are 10f, 10g for feminine attributes and 10b and 10c for masculine attributes. The remaining attributes of question 10 should simply support the tendency of the calculated index score.

The index formula for Uncertainty Avoidance is formulated by Hofstede *et al.* (2008a) as the following:

$$UAI = 40(m20 - m16) + 25(m24 - m27) + C(ua) \qquad (3)$$

This formula is similar to the MAS index formula, only with different weighting factors. The questions m20 and m24 indicate low UA attributes, whereas m16 and m27 indicate high UA attributes. Thus, low UA attributed questions are the minuends of the difference and the high UA attributed questions are the subtrahends. Regarding the criticism of Hofstede and the criticised validity of the questions, question m20 was exchanged, whereas the other indicator questions were adopted from the VSM08. The question m20 asks for the 'state of health in these days' with an answer range from very good to very poor (Hofstede *et al.*, 2008b). The decision to exchange this question was due to the doubt of its validity and reliability, as the question is very broad, its purpose is not clear and it is asked at a specific point in time. A respondent is likely to answer this question differently at a different time and is implicating a subject and participant error, as for example: a student would probably answer this question differently in the first lecture in the morning or in the last one late in the evening. Therefore, the question was exchanged with another low UA attributed question Hofstede calls 'Employment stability' as this is a way of avoiding uncertainty (Hofstede, 2001). Here respondents are asked to rate the duration of the working period they would like to work for the company they are at the moment. This question was adjusted and varied, due to the fact that the respondents were students and are not working for a company at this point. Thus, the resulting index formula of the UAI is:

$$UAI = 40(m2 - m1) + 25(m5 - m3) + C(ua) \qquad (4)$$

These two indices are further analysed in Section 4.3 and 4.4.

The questionnaire in total has 18 questions, where 8 questions indicate UA, 2 questions MAS and 8 demographic questions. Question 10, which indicates MAS, is further divided into 8 attributes to analyse the dimension. Out of the 8 UA questions and 8 MAS attributes plus 1 extra MAS question, 4 questions are each required to calculate the indices. The remaining questions can be referred as 'Check Questions' and offer further, clearer and deeper analysis of the dimensions and more detailed characteristics, which are essential to analyse the dimension more profound as it is done in Section 4.3.2 and 4.4.2. All questions have different dimension attributes and are coded as 'mas' or 'fem' or 'high UA' or 'low UA' questions. The pre-coding of 1-5 is dependent on the attributed questions, which is always characterised with 1 while the opposite character is then 5. For example, a masculine attributed question is coded 1-5, where 1 is masculine and 5 is feminine. Vice versa, a feminine attributed question is coded 1-5, where 1 is feminine and 5 is masculine. This is the same case for UA.

4.3 MASCULINITY

In this section the MAS Index Score is calculated and compared to Hofstede's (1980) MAS scores. Furthermore, additionally attributes are analysed within the findings of the survey.

Hofstede *et al.* (2010) distinguish between the feminine and masculine pole, where the importance of good relationship with the manager, cooperation, living area and employment security are creating the feminine pole and the importance of earnings, challenge, recognition and advancement the masculine pole.

4.3.1 MAS Index Score

The modified MAS dimension index formula was derived from Hofstede's VSM Manual 08 (Hofstede *et al.*, 2008a) like explained above and resulted in the following formula:

$$MAS = 35(m10f - m10b) + 35(m10g - m10c) + C(mf) \qquad (5)$$

Calculating the score for each country with this formula results in the following product of equation:

TABLE XV:

THIS STUDY MAS EQUATION

Germany- MAS				UK- MAS			
mean Question 10f	(Q.5)	2,22		mean Question 10f	(Q.5)	2,17
mean Question 10b	(Q.3)	2,32		mean Question 10b	(Q.3)	2,04
mean Question 10g	(Q.8)	2,41		mean Question 10g	(Q.8)	2,11
mean Question 10c	(Q.10)	2,09		mean Question 10c	(Q.10)	1,82
Consant (C)		50		Constant (C)		50
MAS=35*(m05-m03)+35*(m08-m10)+C MAS=35*(m10f–m10b)+35*(m10g–m10c) +C		57,26		MAS=35*(m05-m03)+35*(m08-m10)+C MAS=35*(m10f–m10b)+35*(m10g–m10c)+C		64,60

In this equation Constant (C) is 50, as C is a positive or negative constant that is dependent on the sample nature, which further is not influencing the comparison of the two countries (Hofstede *et al.*, 2008a). As the result of the equation of both countries is positive, it means that the cultures are masculine.

Vice versa, a negative outcome would indicate that a culture is feminine. Therefore, the scores are positioned over 50, to demonstrate more conveniently that these countries are masculine. Including the constant, the comparison of the MAS dimension of Germany and UK is more convenient and a difference arose.

TABLE XVI:

THIS STUDY'S MAS COMPARED WITH HOFSTEDE'S MAS

	Germany	UK
This study MAS score	57	65
Hofstede MAS score	66	66

According to the personal calculated MAS dimension score, Germany has a score of 57 and the UK 65. While Hofstede *et al.* (2010) claims, that Germany and UK score similarly with a score of 66, this study reveals that UK scores are actually higher and is even a more masculine country than Germany. To analyse the gap of the MAS dimension scores the indicator questions 10f), 10b), 10g) and 10c) which are defined by Hofstede, are analysed in more detail. Additionally, significant check questions are analysed as well to see in how far they support the personal MAS score.

Question 10f) is a feminine attributed question and is asking for the importance of 'Cooperation' and in how far it is important for the respondent to cooperate well with colleagues (Hofstede *et al.*, 2010). According to the survey, the mean answer of both countries is 'very important'. With a mean of 2,2, (1= utmost important, 5= very little important) Germany and the UK score relatively high on this feminine characteristic question.

Question 10f) Cooperation

Category	Germany	UK
utmost important	23%	19%
very important	42%	53%
moderate	28%	19%
little importance	7%	7%
very little importance	1%	1%
Do not know	0%	0%

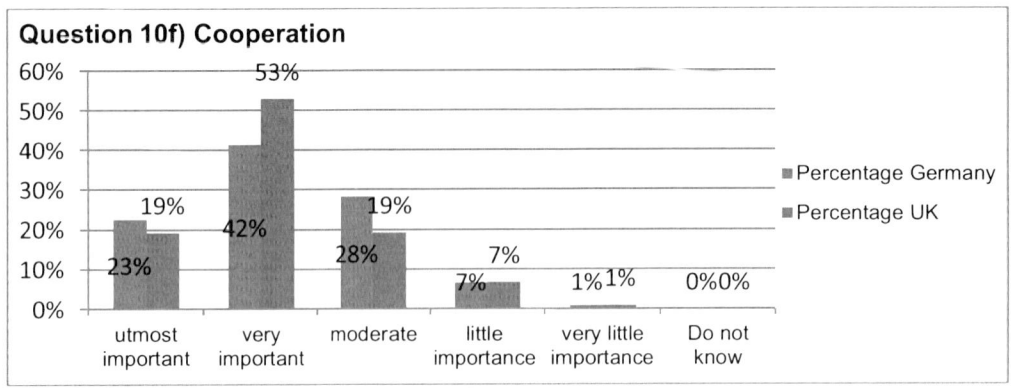

FIGURE 10: QUESTION 10F) COOPERATION

Question 10b) is a masculine attributed question and aims to identify the individual importance of the respondents towards 'Recognition' (Hofstede *et al.*, 2010). For UK students 'Recognition' in an ideal job, is a little more important than for German students, as with an average of 2,0 UK scores very masculine. Even though, German students scores very masculine as well with an average of 2,3, 20% of the UK students think recognition is 'utmost important' and even 58% rated it as 'very important'. However, 42% of German students think that Recognition is of 'moderate' and 6% of 'little importance', while 53% rate it as 'very' or of 'utmost important' compared to 79% of the British students.

Question 10b) Recognition

Category	Germany	UK
utmost important	21%	20%
very important	32%	59%
moderate	42%	19%
little importance	6%	1%
very little importance	0%	1%
Do not know	0%	0%

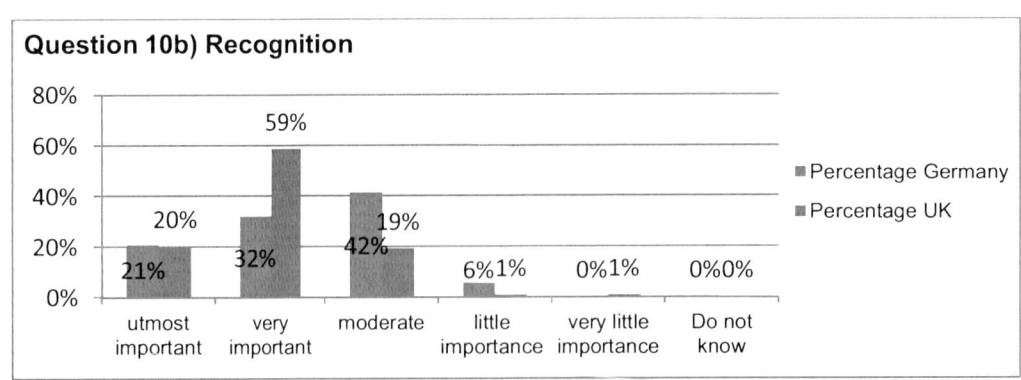

FIGURE 11: QUESTION 10B) RECOGNITION

The Question 10g) is asking about the importance to 'live in an area desirable' (Hofstede *et al.*, 2010, p.139) to the respondent and his/ her family and is another feminine attributed question. UK students rated its importance on average relatively high, as 33% think the 'Living Area' is of 'utmost important' and even 34% think it is 'very important'. As a result, 67% of the UK students think this factor is 'very' or 'utmost important', while only 53% of the German students think so. A relative high proportion of the German participants rated the living area as a 'moderate' importance and even 13% think it only has 'little importance'.

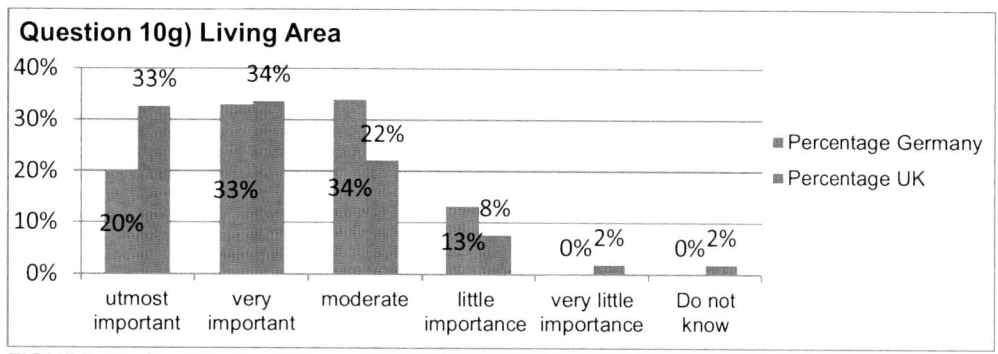

FIGURE 12: QUESTION 10G) LIVING AREA

The last indicator question, which is necessary to calculate the MAS score, according to Hofstede *et al.* (2008a) is Question 10c). This question wants to know the participant's opinion about the importance of the opportunity of 'Advancement' in an ideal job (Hofstede *et al.*, 2010). This is another masculine attribute and UK scores with an average of 1,8 relative highly masculine, while Germany reaches an average of 2,1.

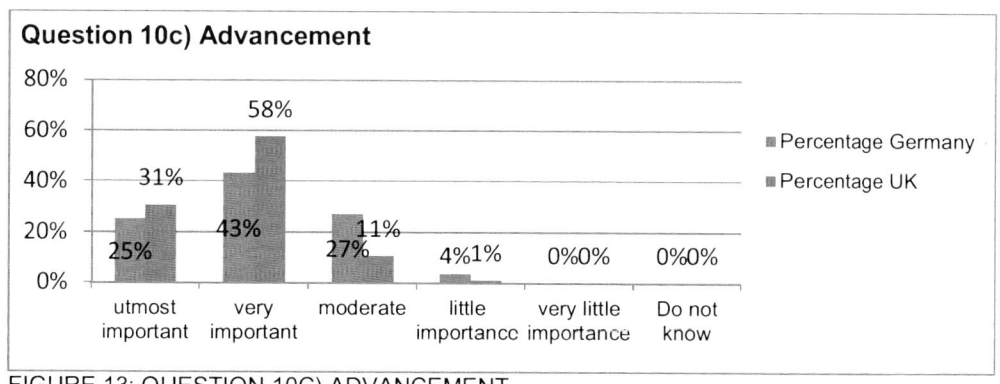

FIGURE 13: QUESTION 10C) ADVANCEMENT

Putting all the Indicator Question together results in the following Graph:

Averages of Indicator Questions

Question	Germany	UK
Question 10b (Q.3) — Masculinity (1=mas; 5=fem)	2,3	2,0
Question 10c (Q.10) — Masculinity (1=mas; 5=fem)	2,1	1,8
Question 10f (Q.5) — Femininity (1=fem; 5=mas)	2,2	2,2
Question 10g (Q.8) — Femininity (1=fem; 5=mas)	2,4	2,1

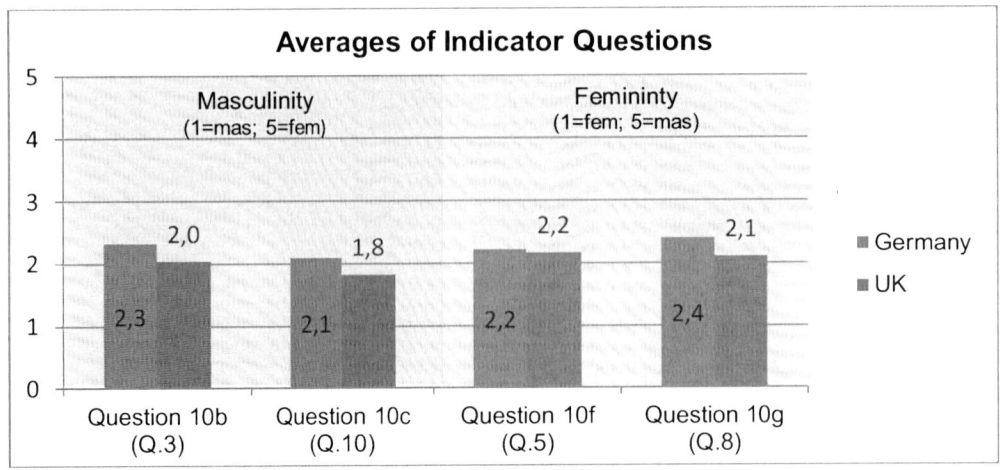

FIGURE 14: AVERAGES OF INDICATOR QUESTIONS

This graphs shows the indicator questions divided into Masculinity and Femininity attributed questions. Here it can be seen, that UK scores more masculine on the masculine attributes than Germany. Even though UK scores a bit higher on the feminine attributes as well, the masculine attributes are outbalancing them. With scores of 65 for UK and 57 for Germany, the UK is, using Hofstede's *et al.* (2008a) dimension calculation, more masculine than Germany. While analysing these indicator questions, the question arose, why Hofstede *et al.* (2008a) exactly chose these questions? He never justifies his choice, he only states that these questions are necessary to compute the scores (Hofstede *et al.*, 2008a). Further he states, that the other questions 'were included for experimental use' (Hofstede *et al.*, 2008a., p.12). However, it is not really clear why these four questions are more important than the others. Looking at all the feminine and masculine attributed questions together actually shows that the differences overall are not that high (Figure 15 and 16). On the masculine attributed questions, UK (2,0) scores more masculine than Germany (2,1), while on the feminine attributed questions UK (2,2) scores more feminine than Germany (2,3). However, the difference of the countries is with 0,2 the same, which actually would support Hofstede's (2001) view that Germany and the UK are similar masculine countries.

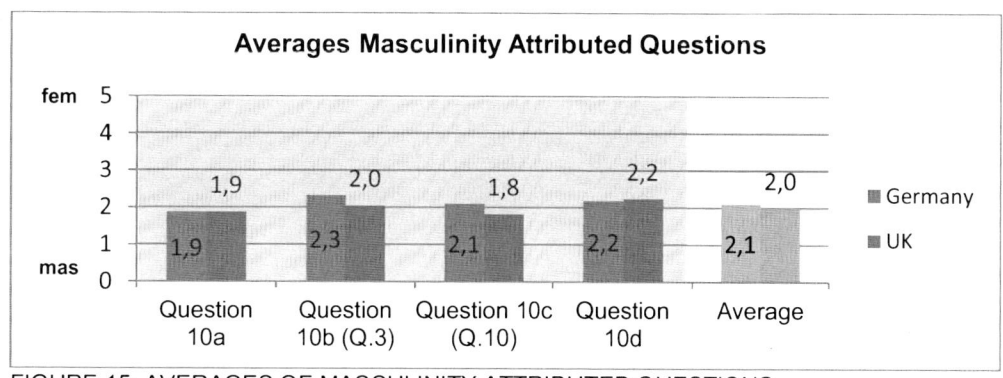

FIGURE 15: AVERAGES OF MASCULINITY ATTRIBUTED QUESTIONS

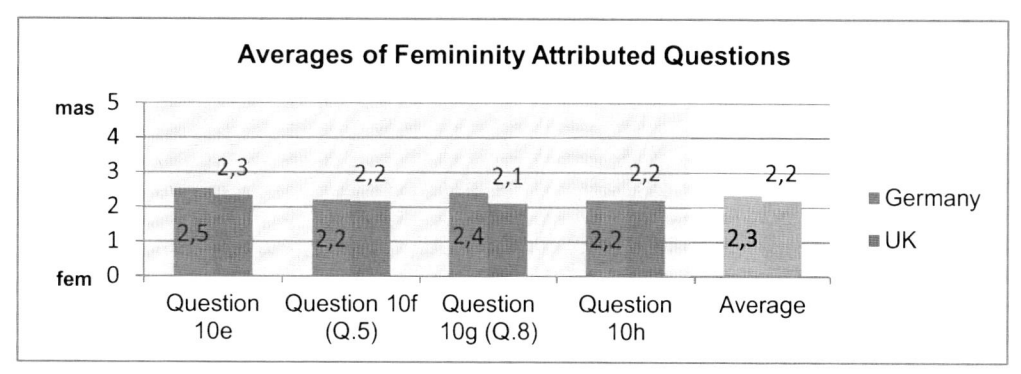

FIGURE 16: AVERAGES OF FEMININITY ATTRIBUTED QUESTIONS

But, Hofstede *et al.* (2008a) only picked four of these questions and calculated out of them the MAS dimension score, where a different result was concluded. However, it might be significant to include all of these questions to increase its informational value.

4.3.2 Further Analysis

One explanation of the Personal MAS score difference can be the gender distribution of the participants, which is shown in Figure 17. While in Germany, the less masculine country according to the personal score, 58% of the respondents were female and 42% male, the opposite was the case in the UK, 58% male and 42% female participants. However, Hofstede *et al.* (2010) and Jones (2007) claim that the dimension does not refer to the gender

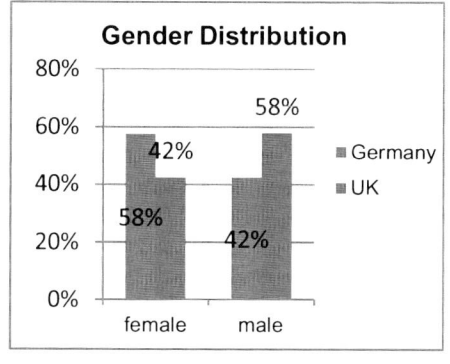

FIGURE 17: GENDER DISTRIBUTION

75

dominance, but more to the degree to which masculine or feminine characteristics are given. Despite this, seeking for an explanation of the detected difference a test is made to calculate a gender dimension score for each country. This reveals that German male student score 67 on the MAS dimension and female students 50. Comparing this to the UK shows that female UK students score higher than their German counterparts with a score of 63. The male 'Personal' Gender MAS score of 65 does not differ too much from its female complement (Table XVII).

TABLE XVII:

CALCULATED GENDER MAS

	Calculated Gender MAS	
	male	female
Germany	67,11	50,00
UK	65,36	63,60

According to the Calculated Gender MAS scores, the gender role differentiation is higher in Germany and with only a slight difference in the UK. Even though UK scores higher, both countries are still very masculine countries where an unequal result of female and male participants is expected, as Hofstede and Hofstede (2009a) states that 'these [masculine] countries show a gap between men's values and women's values'. Hofstede and Hofstede (2009a) state, that women in masculine countries are not as 'masculine' as men and that in feminine countries, women are always relatively more 'feminine'. Further, he claims that women in 'masculine countries [...] are more assertive and more competitive, but not as much as the men' (Hofstede and Hofstede, 2009a, n.p.). This supports the Personal MAS score, as UK female students are more 'masculine' than the German females, but not as 'masculine' as their male complements.

In addition, the Question 9 is analysed to support the MAS dimension scores of the countries. This Check Question asks the participants to rank the most important factors in an ideal job from 1-3. As explained already, this question has some limitations due to its relatively high proportion of invalid answers. However, as only 10% of the sample unit misunderstood this question, it is still meaningful. Here it is interesting to see, that this Check Question supports the personal MAS score in so far, that the UK students tend to rank masculine attributes higher than their German counterparts.

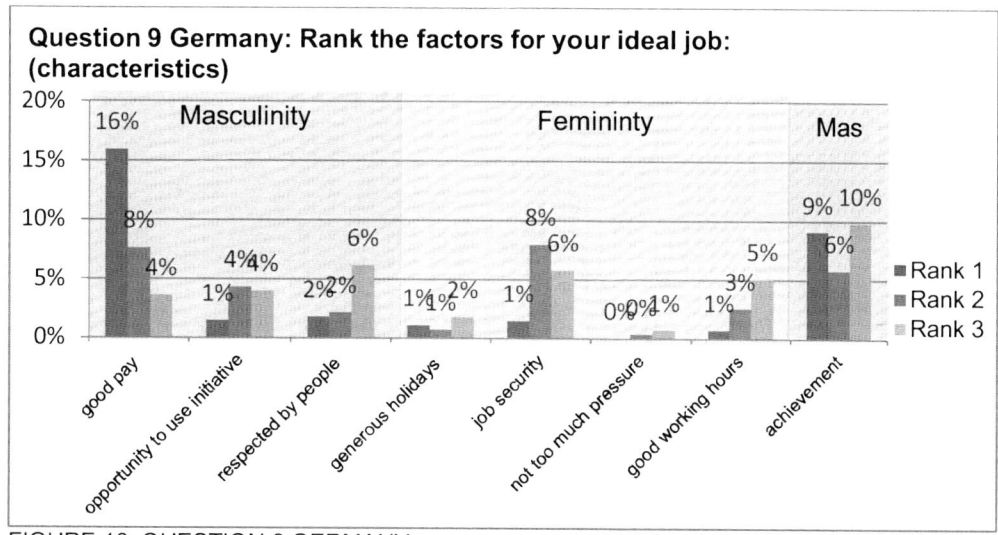

FIGURE 18: QUESTION 9 GERMANY

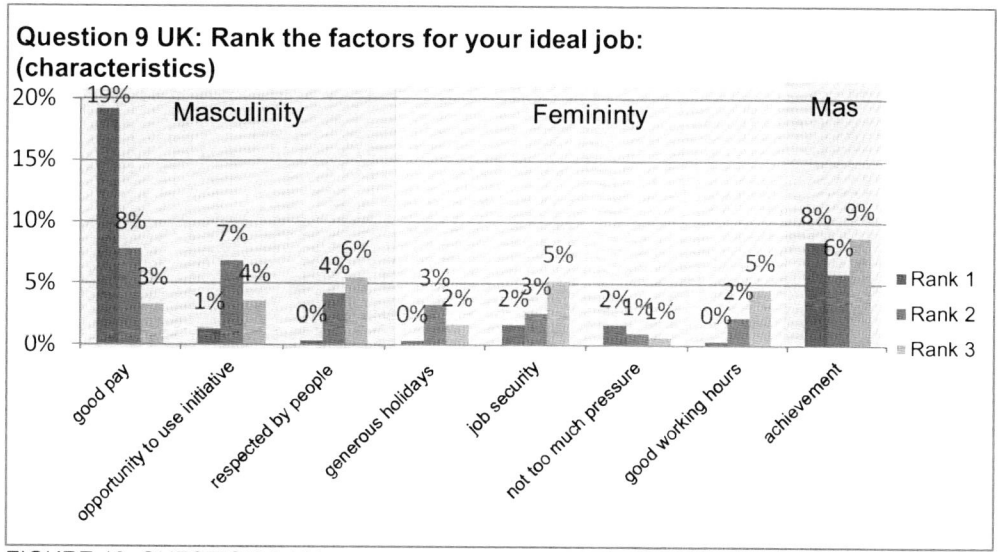

FIGURE 19: QUESTION 9 UK

72% of the German student ranked masculine attributes as their most important factors in an ideal job, while even 75% of the UK students ranked them. On the other hand, 28% of the German and 25% of the UK students ranked feminine attributes under the Top 3. By far the most important factor for the participants is the masculine attribute of 'good pay' and the least important factor is the feminine attribute 'not too much pressure'. While Question 10 is asking about the importance of the attributes, this question makes the statement more clearly by prioritising the attributes. Subsequent, the masculine attributes are clearly outperforming the feminine attributes and it is obvious that Germany and the UK are clearly masculine countries.

4.4 UNCERTAINTY AVOIDANCE

In this section the Personal UA Index Score is calculated and compared to Hofstede's (2001) UA scores. Furthermore, additional attributes are analysed within the findings of the survey.

Uncertainty Avoidance is defined as the 'extent to which the members of a culture feel threatened by ambiguous or unknown situations' (Hofstede *et al.*, 2010, p.191). Further Hofstede explains, that this feeling is 'expressed through nervous stress and in a need for predictability: a need for written or unwritten rules' (Hofstede *et al.*, 2010, p.191).

4.4.1 UA Index Score

The modified UA dimension index formula was derived from Hofstede's *et al.* (2008a) VSM Manual 08 as well and resulted in the following formula:

$$UAI = 40(m2 - m1) + 25(m5 - m3) + C(ua) \qquad (6)$$

Calculating the score for each country with this formula results in the following product of the equation:

TABLE XVIII:

THIS STUDY UA EQUATION

Germany - UAI			UK - UAI		
mean Question 2	(Q.20)	1,93	mean Question 2	(Q.20)	1,70
mean Question 1	(Q.16)	3,64	mean Question 1	(Q.16)	3,16
mean Question 5	(Q.24)	2,12	mean Question 5	(Q.24)	2,94
mean Question 3	(Q.27)	2,85	mean Question 3	(Q.27)	3,11
Constant (C)		100	Constant (C)		100
UAI=40*(m20-m16)+25*(m24-m27)+C UAI = 40(m2 - m1) + 25(m5 – m3) + C		13,22	UAI=40*(m20-m16)+25*(m24-m27)+C UAI = 40(m2 - m1) + 25(m5 – m3) + C		37,32

A negative result means a low UA characteristically culture and a positive result means a high UA culture. As both equations have a negative output, the Constant of 100 was added to shift the UAI scores between 0 and 100 and to demonstrate more conveniently the low UA characteristic of these countries (Hofstede *et al.*, 2008a). Comparing the Personal UA score with Hofstede's (2001) UA score reveals an opposite outcome.

TABLE XIX:

THIS STUDY'S UA COMPARED WITH HOFSTEDE'S UA

	Germany	UK
This study UA score	13	37
Hofstede UA score	65	35

While Hofstede (2001) claims that Germany has a score of 65 and has a higher UAI than UK with 35, this study argues that the UK actually has a higher UAI than Germany. Even though the scores cannot be compared directly with Hofstede's (1980), it is interesting that in this study the opposite of Hofstede's (1980) finding is the case. Furthermore, it can be said that actually both countries are low UA cultures, according to the findings of this study and that Germany is not as high UA as expected from Hofstede's findings.

To analyse this further in detail, the indicator questions, which are needed, according to Hofstede *et al.* (2008a) for calculating the UAI are introduced and analysed.

Question 2 is a low UA attributed question and is asking for the time of duration the respondent thinks to work for at the first company they are employed at. This question is labeled by Hofstede (2001, p.149) 'Employment stability' and is one way of avoiding uncertainty. As Germany is, according to Hofstede (2001) a high UA country, it was expected that German students would want to stay longer in a company than UK students, due to their desire of creating certainty. This is partly supported by this survey, as 47% of the German students think they will stay 'from two to five years', but eventually even 44% of the UK students think the same. Even though, Germany scores clearly higher in Hofstede's (2001) score. 30% of the UK participants answer they want to stay 'two years at most', which shows no fear from the uncertainty according to Hofstede (2001). Also 15% of the German students show a low UA characteristic.

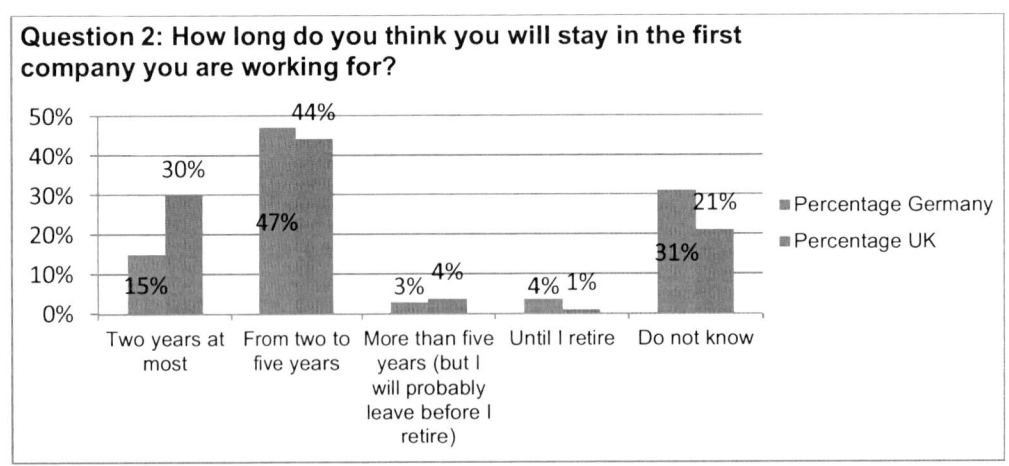

FIGURE 20: QUESTION 2

Question 1 is a high UA attributed questions and is asking about the stress occurrence of the participants. Hofstede *et al.* (2010, p.190) gives the example that 'British employees always scored less nervous than German employees, be they managers, engineers, secretaries, or unskilled factory workers'.

However, this survey states that it is actually the other way around. Looking at the chart below it can be clearly seen that UK students feel more nervous or tensed than German students. 13% of UK participants are 'Usually' feeling this way and 53% feel 'Sometimes' nervous. 52% German participants on the other hand are feeling only 'Seldom' this way and only 29% 'Sometimes'.

Question 1: How often do you feel nervous or tense at university?

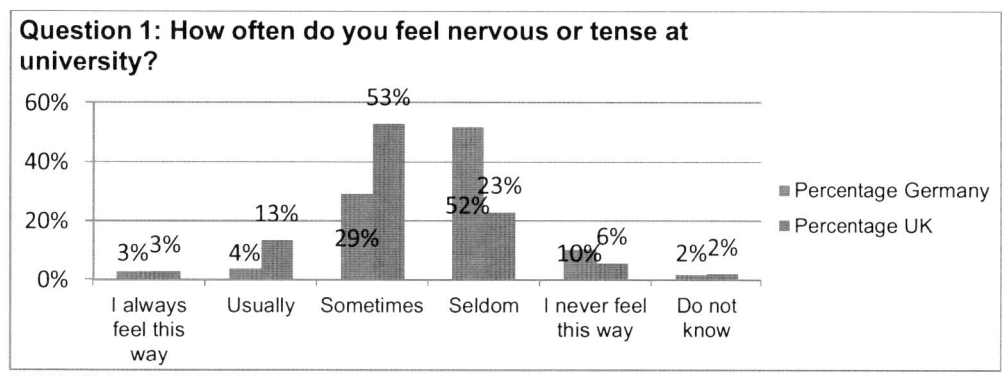

Response	Percentage Germany	Percentage UK
I always feel this way	3%	3%
Usually	4%	13%
Sometimes	29%	53%
Seldom	52%	23%
I never feel this way	10%	6%
Do not know	2%	2%

FIGURE 21: QUESTION 1

Question 5 is a low UA attributed question and is asking to agree to a statement about their teacher's knowledge. Low UA countries accept it, when their teachers say 'I do not know', while in high UA cultures a teacher is supposed to have 'all the answers' (Hofstede *et al.*, 2010). Expected from this knowledge, British students should accept their teacher's saying 'I do not know' while German students should expect their teachers to know everything. However, it is the other way around again and 71% of the German participants think that it is ok, if their teachers may say 'I do not know', while only 49% of the British students say so. On the other side, 46% of British participants want their teachers to have 'all the answers' and only 27% of the German counterparts want the same. While Germany shows a high tendency towards 'may say I do not know', the UK results are more balanced. According

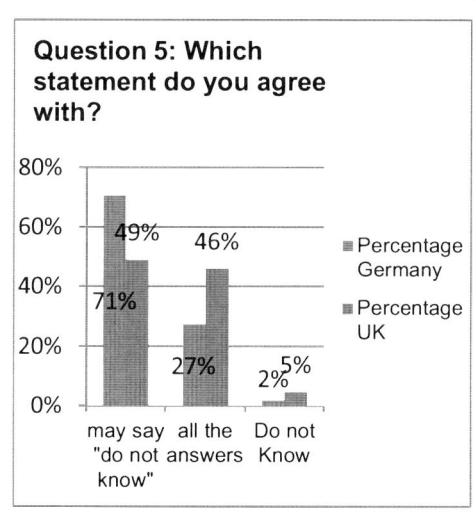

Question 5: Which statement do you agree with?

Response	Percentage Germany	Percentage UK
may say "do not know"	71%	49%
all the answers	27%	46%
Do not Know	2%	5%

FIGURE 22: QUESTION 5

to the answers of this question Germany seems to be a lower UA country than the UK.

The last indicator question is question 3, which is another high UA attributed question and is labeled by Hofstede (2001, p.148) 'rule orientation'. The participants are asked in how far they agree to the following statement: 'Company rules should not be broken- even when the employee thinks it is in the company's best interest'. Hofstede *et al.* (2010) states, that law, rules and regulations are preventing uncertainties in societies, which are more welcomed in high UA countries where people 'have been programmed since early childhood to feel comfortable in structured environments' (p.209). People are more rule-oriented and it is not acceptable to break a company's rule under any circumstances. Low UA cultures are programmed vice versa, and it is alright to break a company's rules as long as it is for the company's best interest. As according to Hofstede (2001), Germany is a high and UK a low UA country- hence Germans are expected to agree, while British are expected to disagree to the statement. This is supported by this study, as 23% of the German participants 'agree' and even 5% 'strongly agree', while 28% of British students 'disagree' and even 5% 'strongly disagree'. However, the majority of the students is undecided about this statement and cannot make a clear agreement or disagreement.

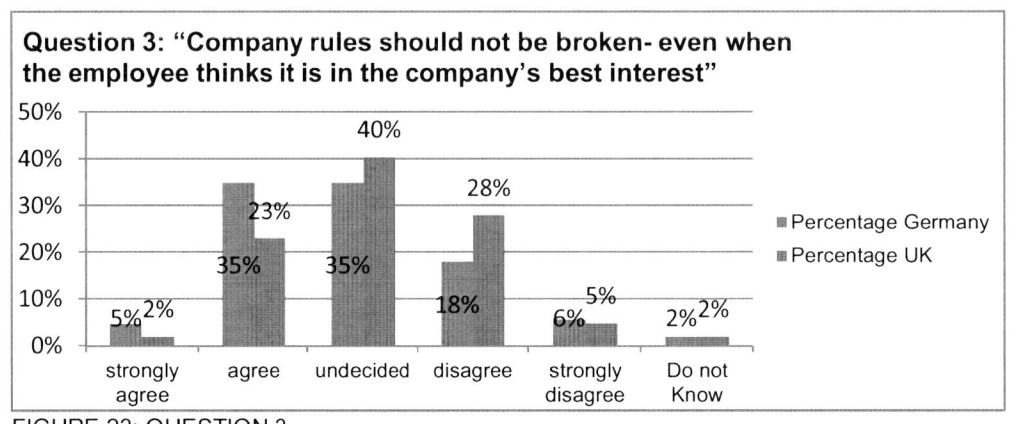

FIGURE 23: QUESTION 3

Assembling all the indicator questions results in the following chart:

UA Indicator Questions

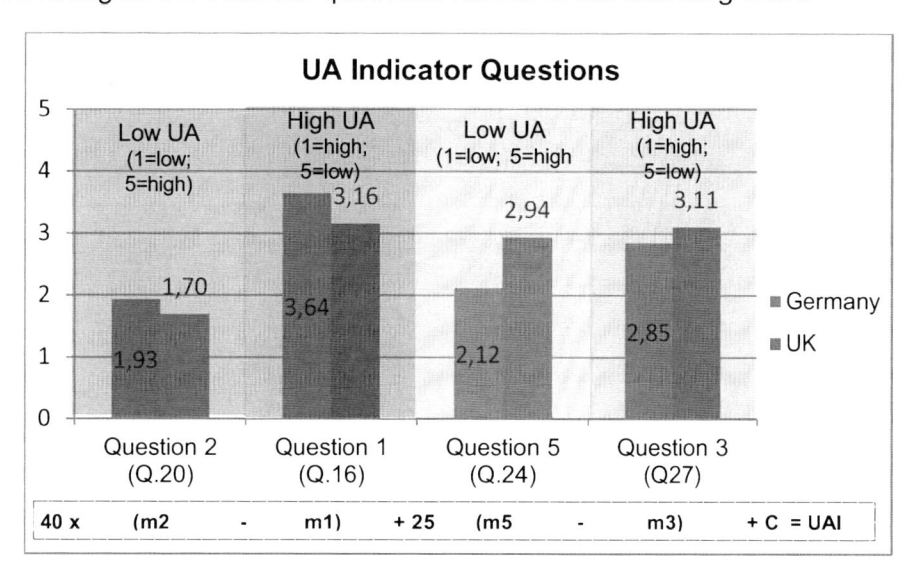

	Question 2 (Q.20)	Question 1 (Q.16)	Question 5 (Q.24)	Question 3 (Q27)
	Low UA (1=low; 5=high)	High UA (1=high; 5=low)	Low UA (1=low; 5=high)	High UA (1=high; 5=low)
Germany	1,70	3,16	2,94	3,11
UK	1,93	3,64	2,12	2,85

40 x (m2 - m1) + 25 (m5 - m3) + C = UAI

FIGURE 24: UA INDICATOR QUESTIONS

On the first sight, UK does not seem higher in the UAI than Germany, as actually it seems balanced. However, the average of the high UA attributed Indicator questions is 3,25 for Germany and 3,13 for UK. UK seems higher in UAI (1=high UA) here, because it is closer to 1, however, both seem to be low UAI countries. The average of the low attributed Indicator questions is 2,02 for Germany and 2,32 for the UK, which means that Germany has a lower UA than UK (1= low UA). The difference of the first term (m2-m1) is smaller for Germany (1,93-3,64= -1,71) than for the UK (1,7-3,16= -1,46). The difference of the second term (m5-m3) for UK (2,94-3,11= -0,17) and for Germany (2,12-2,85= -0,73) is negative as well, which supports the low UAI for both countries and the tendencies as Germany has a lower score than UK. Further, Question 1 and 2 are weighted higher, with a weighting scale of 40, while Question 3 and 5 are weighted with 25. That is why the first two questions are more dominant and influence the result more than the last two questions. Because of that, UK scores in the end significantly higher than Germany, as UK is less (before adding the constant) negative and therefore higher in UAI.

Here applies the same as in the MAS dimension, as Hofstede *et al.* (2008a) does not really justify the choice of question and he does not really explain his weighting factors. He decided that some questions are more dominant than others. But looking at all the questions together, a different conclusion could be made.

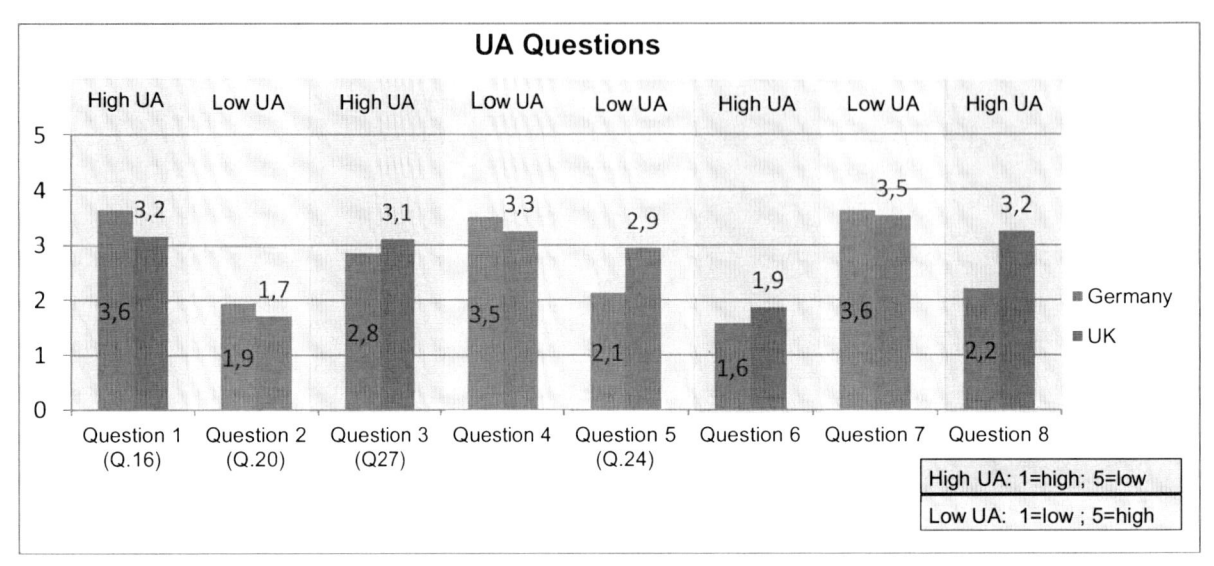

FIGURE 25: UA QUESTIONS

Dividing the questions into high UA and low UA attributed questions results in the graphs shown on the next page.

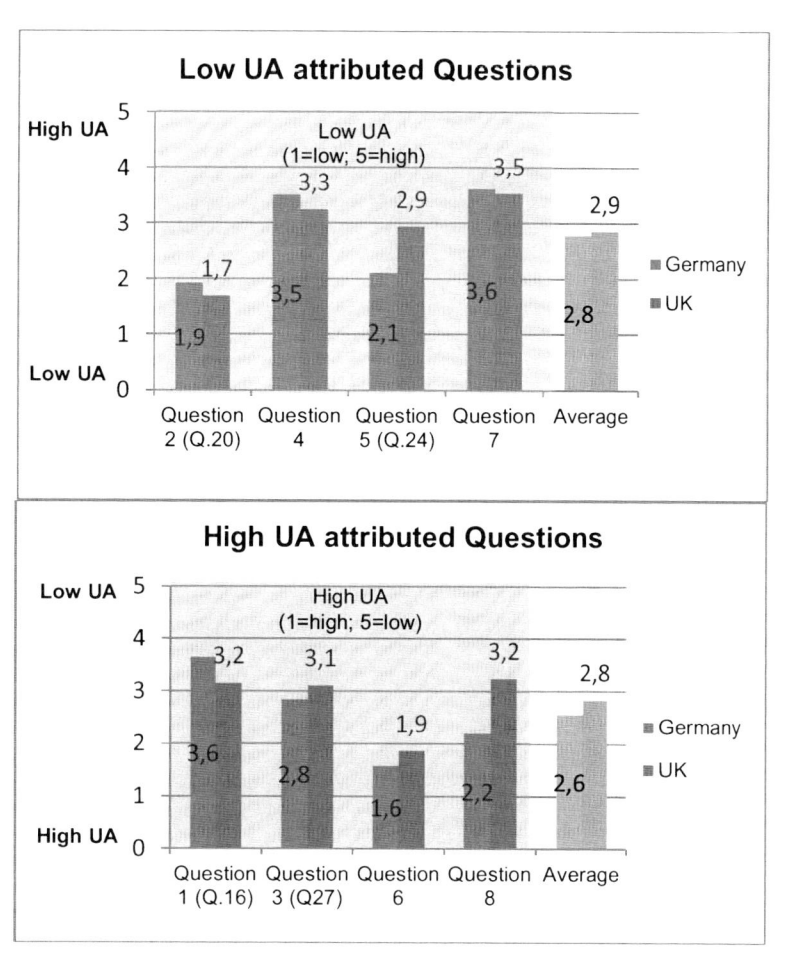

FIGURE 26: HIGH AND LOW UA QUESTIONS

The average of the low UA attributed questions shows, that the average for Germany is here 2,8 and for the UK 2,9, which means that Germany is a bit lower in UA than UK here. On the other side, the average of the high UA attributed questions for Germany is 2,6 and for the UK 2,8. This means that if taken all the averages of the high UA attributed questions together, without any weighting, than Germany has a higher UA than UK. Taking both averages together (Ø Low UA – Ø High UA) contradicts the personal calculated UAI for the countries, as Germany (2,8-2,6= 0,2) seems now to have a higher UA than the UK (2,9-2,8= 0,1). Therefore, it is to say again that it depends on the chosen questions by Hofstede *et al.* (2008a) on how the result is going to look like. If actually the averages would have been taken, than Hofstede's (2001) tendencies could have been supported, but with the chosen questions and the personal calculated UA score it does not. The further analysis will introduce other questions of the survey, which support this view that the averages of the questions of this study do not support Hofstede's (2001) view of Germany having a higher UA than the UK.

4.4.2 Further Analysis

'Most Germans, for example, favoured structured learning situation with precise objectives, detailed assignments, and strict timetables' (Hofstede *et al.*, 2010, p.205). Further, Hofstede *et al.* (2010, p.205) claims that 'Most British participants, on the other hand, despised too much structure. They liked open-ended learning situations with vague objectives, broad assignments, and no timetables at all'. Hofstede *et al.* (2010) gives these examples of typical low and high UA countries and distinguishes between structure loving Germans and structure disliking British. Therefore, a clear distinction between Germany and the UK was expected in the structure related questions 4, 6 and 8. However, the clear differentiation failed to appear within this study. Even though, 40% of UK students preferred 'open ended learning situations', 52% favoured 'structured learning situations'. This question 4 is a low UA attributed questions and according to it, both countries tend to be high UA cultures. As expected, the majority (58%) of the German participants favoured 'structured learning situations'. However, 34% actually prefer 'open ended learning situations'.

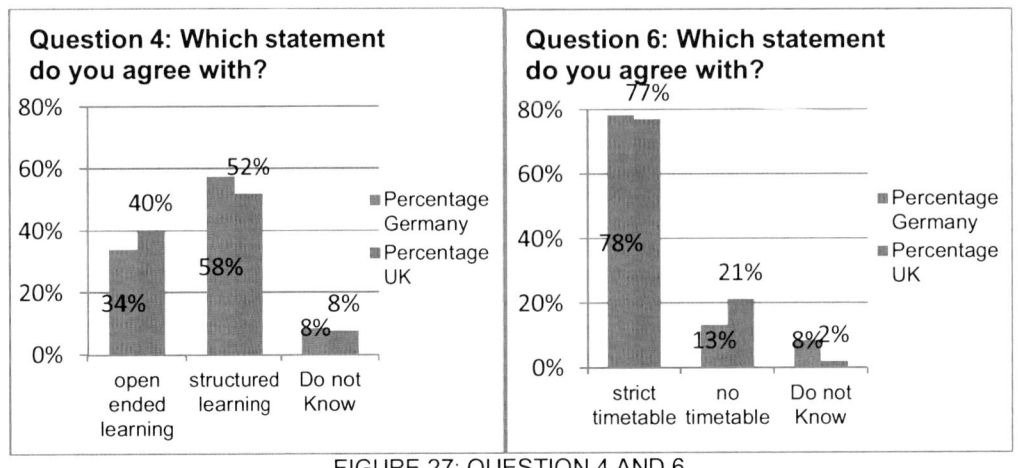

FIGURE 27: QUESTION 4 AND 6

Further, Hofstede *et al.* (2010) states, that most Germans favour strict timetables and most British favour no timetable. Although more UK participants prefer 'no timetable' compared to Germans, the majority of both countries favour a 'strict timetable'. Question 6 is another high UA attributed questions and according to the answers, Germany and the UK show high UA characteristics.

Moreover, question 8 is another high UA attributed question and is a Check Question for question 3, as it asks for structure and rules. Question 3 already showed that German students are more rule-oriented than British ones, which is approved by question 8. 66% of German participants prefer a 'structured and rule-dominated environment' while 28% favour an 'unstructured environment with no more rules than strictly necessary'. The majority of British students (54%) prefer the 'unstructured environment'; however, even 42% favour the 'structured environment'.

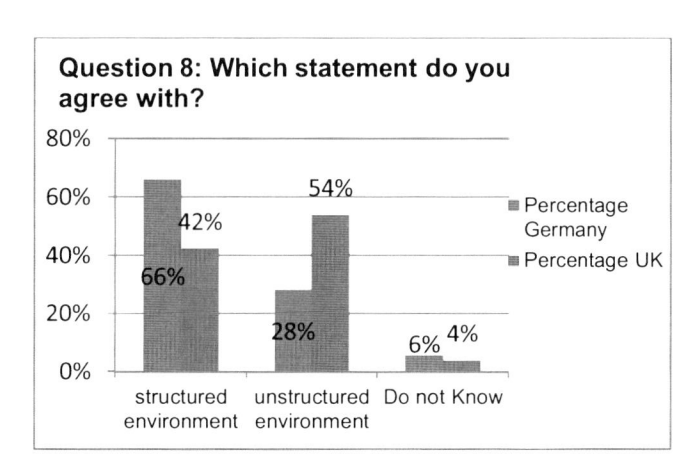

FIGURE 28: QUESTION 8

Furthermore, the item of 'Job Security' in question 9 could be used as a check question for question 2, which was labelled 'Employment stability' (Figure 29). More German students wanted to stay a longer period at the first company they are going to work for than the British student. This is supported by the ranking question of the 'Job Security' item, as more German students ranked this item under the three ranks.

Job Security

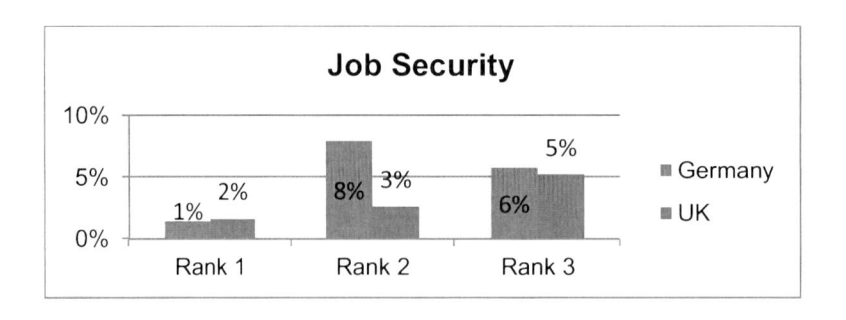

(Chart showing: Rank 1: Germany 1%, UK 2%; Rank 2: Germany 8%, UK 3%; Rank 3: Germany 6%, UK 5%)

FIGURE 29: JOB SECURITY

Moreover, Hofstede *et al.* (2010, p.191) states that 'if in a country more people felt under stress at work, in the same country more people wanted rules to be respected, and more people wanted to have a long-term career'. This is again not the case for this small replication study. While more UK students feel more under stress in university, more German participants wanted rules to be respected and a long-term career.

4.5 DISCUSSION

The Hypotheses that have been derived from the literature review substantiated the process of the analysis of the primary research. Personal dimension scores were calculated in the same way Hofstede *et al.* (2008a) did. These personal scores are the source of evaluating the Hypotheses. The first Hypothesis was:

H_1: The cultural dimension of Masculinity/ Femininity has not changed over time and Germany and UK are still very masculine countries with similar scores (66).

The Hypothesis 1 is not supported by the finding of this study, as the MAS tendency has changed here. Even though Germany and the UK are still very masculine countries, the presented study implied that the UK is even more masculine than Germany. These scores are not to be understood as absolute but relative scores. Hence the main statement of the presented findings regarding the MAS dimension is, that the UK is more masculine than Germany.

TABLE XX:

THIS STUDY'S MAS COMPARED TO HOFSTEDE'S MAS

	Germany	UK
This study MAS score	57	65
Hofstede MAS score	66	66

The second hypothesis referring to the UA dimension was:

H_2: The cultural dimension of Uncertainty Avoidance has not changed over time and Germany still scores higher (65) than the UK (35).

The second Hypothesis 2 is not supported by the results either, because the findings of the personal UAI contradict with the findings from Hofstede's (2001) findings. While Hofstede (2001) states that Germany is a high UA and UK a low UA country, this study resulted in the opposite conclusion. According to this study Germany and UK seem to be low UA countries and Germany even lower than the UK.

TABLE XXI:

THIS STUDY'S UA COMAPRED TO HOFSTEDE'S UA

	Germany	UK
This study UA score	13	37
Hofstede UA score	65	35

The statements that are made are based on the personal replication study and the findings that resulted from it. These statements and the study should be handled with caution as they are concerning Hofstede's (1980) original study and compare their findings with his findings. Even though Hofstede's (1980) study is challenged and criticised, this study does not indicate that his findings are wrong or false, because they differ from this study in the matching sample. However, it can be summarised that this replication study is not supporting his findings, but is supporting his way of getting to the findings. Hofstede made an incredible attempt and effort by developing these dimensions and revolutionising the study of cultural differences. Even though there are still some unclear parts concerning the calculation of the score, like the process of choosing the indicator questions or the weighting scale, the overall idea and theoretical approach is one of a kind. Moreover, the reasons for the shift of dimension scores are unclear and many suggestions and speculations could be made, but would not have any sufficient proof.

As Hofstede (1980) did not have the intention to develop these cultural dimensions in the first place, the questions can be said to be not totally valid. However, after he explored the immense finding of the cultural dimensions, he could have adjusted the questions. While calculating and analysing the dimension scores, the main difficulty was the pre-coding, which was adopted from Hofstede's *et al.* (2008) VSM08. While the pre-coding of Hofstede's (VSM08) questionnaire is always 1-5 and the attribute of the question always change, it would be easier and more convenient to change the coding. Having replicated the whole study, it can be recommended that for example 1 stands for feminine and 5 for masculine. This way the averages could have been calculated and already indicate a statement about the degree of MAS.

CHAPTER 5

5 CONCLUSION AND RECOMMENDATIONS

In the following section the key findings and the indications of this study are summarised and concluded. Finally, recommendations for further research are outlined.

5.1 CONCLUSION

Due to globalisation and changing global markets, cross-cultural managements is gaining in importance, hence understanding and managing cultural differences is becoming a 'key' to success. Within his study Hofstede (1980) offers a model of cultural dimension to make cultural differences more feasible and discussable and to prevent cross-cultural business failures. His study is widely used in global operating organisations within trainings and workshops to make employees aware of their own culture and the host country's culture as the first step of effective cross-cultural management is the awareness of the existence of cultural differences as domestic strategies might fail in host countries.

The literature review in Chapter 2 came to the conclusion that, even though, Hofstede's (1980) cultural study is one of the most important ones and widely known, there are many other cultural studies, which are partly supporting his study. The GLOBE project is assumed to be the contemporary, intensified and broader version of Hofstede's cultural dimension, even though its applicability is more complex than Hofstede's (1980) study. There is not only one best approach of studying culture and cultural differences, as there are many ways of doing so. For each and every model of cultural identifications aroused praise and criticism and Hofstede was not spared by criticism. Table XXIII shows the main arguments for and against Hofstede's (1980) study summarised, which were elaborated and discussed within this study.

TABLE XXII:

ARGUMENTS FOR AND AGAINST HOFSTEDE'S STUDY

Arguments for Hofstede (1980)	Arguments against Hofstede (1980)
Relevance	Reliability and Validity of Methodology
Rigour	One Company Approach
Relative Accuracy	National Divisions
Simplicity	Political Influences
	Out-dated
	Too few dimensions
	Culturally biased
	Ecological Fallacy

(Source: Own illustration)

The main criticisms refer to the methodology Hofstede (1980) used and many authors questioned its validity and reliability, as he did not had the intention to develop these cultural dimensions. Another major critique is that the nearly 40-years old survey findings are out-dated and not of any modern value anymore. Addressing these major criticisms, a personal replication study within the two countries of Germany and the UK was undertaken to evaluate the validity and reliability in the 21st century. Further, while obtaining primary data and analysing these, Hofstede's (1980) methodology was assessed and evaluated. The findings of this study and a comparison with Hofstede's (1980) findings can be summarised as shown in Table XXIV.

TABLE XXIII:

THIS STUDY'S FINDINGS

	Germany	UK
This study MAS score	57	65
Hofstede MAS score	66	66
This study UA score	13	37
Hofstede UA score	65	35

Both hypotheses that were established within this study were not supported by the findings, as according to this study the tendencies of the MAS and UA scores have changed. Hofstede claims, that Germany and the UK are masculine countries, which is supported by this study. However, Hofstede further states, that the two countries score similarly on the MAS dimensions, which is not supported by this study as the UK scores even more masculine than Germany. A more significant difference between Hofstede's findings and this study's findings arose within the UA dimension. Hofstede argues that Germany scores significantly higher on the UA than the UK. In this study it is the opposite way, as both countries score low on the UA and Germany even lower than the UK. These assumptions are made on the basis of the calculated indices within the presented study, which are derived from Hofstede's *et al.* (2008a) VSM08 Manual. The validity of Hofstede's methodology and questions is assumed to be not totally valid due to his missing intention to develop the dimensions. This is assumed to be a limitation as even though the methodology and approaches are criticised, they are adopted and adapted within this study as well.

Concluding from the Literature Review, Hofstede's study is still a solid, reasonable study and widely used, even though some researchers had been accepting and adopting his study too enthusiastically and quickly. While analysing in depth the findings of this study and when dealing with Hofstede's methodology and approaches, some questionable aspects were assumed, like the justification of the indicator questions and the weighting factor scales. Based on this it is suggested, that some adjustments should have been made over time, such as changes within the pre-coding, adjusting the questions or even considering all questions for the calculation of the indices to cover all aspects of the answers.

5.2 FUTURE RESEARCH AND RECOMMENDATION

The on-going debate about cultural changes is still present and while some researchers claim that culture cannot be changed over time, other state it can; however, there is still no significant proof for either side. While this small replication study already showed some new tendencies for two dimensions in only two countries; thus further replication studies with more countries and all dimensions would be appropriate to give evidence for either side of the debate.

The GLOBE project is the closest to give some evidence and proof of this discussion and with continuing longitudinal studies like this, the answer might be found in the near future. Furthermore, cultural researchers could add follow up-interviews and observations to their surveys to increase the reliability and validity by avoiding the use of only one research strategy as Hofstede did.

Moreover, the understanding of the impact of cultural differences on cross-cultural management is a 'key' to success. Therefore organisations should consider implementing cross-cultural teams, which are responsible for identifying cultural differences within home and host countries and develop approaches and strategies to work efficiently across cultural borders.

REFERENCES

Amadeo, K. (2008) *Could the Mortgage Crisis and Bank Bailout Have Been Prevented?* [Online]. About.com: US Economy. Retrieved from: http://useconomy.about.com/od/criticalssues/a/prevent_crisis.htm [Accessed 3 November 2010].

Anderson, V. (2004) *Research Methods in Human Resource Management.* London: CIPD.

Armstrong, A. (2003) *A Handbook of Human Resource Management Practice.* 9th ed. London: Kogan Page.

Bailey, K.D. (1994) *Methods of social research.* 4th ed. New York: The Free Press.

Baskerville, R.F. (2003) 'Hofstede never studied culture', *Accounting, Organization and Society*, Vol. 28, No.1, pp. 1-14.

Baskerville, R.F. (2005) 'A research note: the unfinished business of culture', *Accounting, Organization and Society*, Vol. 30, No. 4, pp. 389-391.

Bhawuk, D.P.S. (2008) 'Globalization and indigenous cultures: Homogenization or differentiation?', *International Journal of Intercultural Relations*, Vol. 32, No. 4, pp. 305-317.

Bing, J.W. (2004) 'Hofstede's consequences: The impact of his work on consulting and business practices', *Academy of Management Executive*, Vol. 18, No.1, pp. 80-87.

Blodgett, J. G., Bakir, A. and Rose, G., M. (2008) 'A test of the validity of Hofstede's cultural framework', *Journal of Consumer Marketing*, Vol. 25, No. 6, pp. 339-349.

Bourguignon, F., Marin, D., Venables, A. J., Winters, A., Giavazzi, F., Coyle, D., Seabright, P., Verdier, T., O'Rourke, K. H., Fernandez, R. and Portes, R. (2002) *Making Sense of Globalization: A guide to the Economic Issues.* London: Center for Economic Policy Research.

Brett, J.M. (2007) *Negotiating globally: How to negotiate deals, resolve disputes, and make decisions across cultural boundaries.* 2nd ed. San Francisco, CA: John Wiley & Sons, Inc.

Brisbane Catholic Education (1998) *A Position Paper on Cultural Literacy and Languages.* Brisbane: Catholic Education Office.

Browne, K. (2005) *An Introduction to Sociology.* 3rd ed. Oxford: Blackwell Publishers.

Bryman, A. and Bell, E. (2003) *Business research methods.* 2nd ed. Oxford: Oxford University Press.

Bulmer, M. (1984) *Sociological Research Methods: An Introduction.* 2nd ed. New Jersey: MacMillan Press.

Carr, S.C. (2004) *Globalization and culture at work: Exploring their Combined Glocality.* Dordrecht: Kluwer Academic Publishers.

Cohen, L., Manion, L. and Morrison, K. (2007) *Research Methods in Education.* 6th ed. Abingdon: Routledge.

Cline, W. R. (2010) *Financial Globalization, Economic Growth, and the Crisis of 2007-09.* Washington: Peterson Institute For International Economics.

Collis, J. and Hussey,R. (2009) *Business Research: A practical guide for undergraduate & postgraduate students.* 3rd ed. Basingstoke: Palgrave Macmillan.

Dawson, B. and Young, L. (2003) 'In defence of Hofstede'. Paper presented at the Conference Proceedings, Adelaide, December.

Dillman, D.A. (2007) *Mail and Internet Surveys: The Tailored Design Method.* 2nd ed. Hoboken: Wiley.

Dochartaigh, N.O. (2002) *The Internet Research Handbook: A Practical Guide for Students and Researchers in the Social Science.* London: Sage Publications.

Dorfman, P.W. and Howell, J.P. (1988) 'Dimensions of national culture and effective leadership patterns: Hofstede revisited', *International Comparative Management*, Vol. 3, pp.127-150.

Fang, T. (2003) 'A Critique of Hofstede's Fifth National Culture Dimension', *International Journal of Cross Cultural Management*, Vol. 3, No. 3, pp. 347-368.

Fernandez, D.R., Carlson, D.S., Stepina, L.P. and Nicholson, J.D. (1997) 'Hofstede's Country Classification 25 Years Later', *The Journal of Social Psychology*, Vol. 137, No. 1, pp. 43-54.

Finocchiaro, M.A. (2008) *The essential Galileo*. Indianapolis: Hackett Publishing.

Fletcher, D. (2000) 'Learning to think global and act local: experiences from the small business sector', *Education and Training*, Vol. 42, pp. 211-219.

Foddy, W. (1994) *Constructing Questions for Interviews and Questionnaires*. Cambridge: University Press.

Fougere, M. and Moulettes, A. (2006) 'Development and Modernity in Hofstede's Cultural Consequences: A postcolonial reading', *Lund Institute of Economic Research*. Part 2.

Francesco, A.M. and Gold, B.A. (2005) *International Organizational Behaviour*. 2nd ed. New Jersey: Pearson Education.

French, R. (2010) *Cross-Cultural Management in Work Organisations*. 2nd ed. London: CIPD.

Fresenius (2010) *Homepage of the University of Applied Science Fresenius* [Online]. Hochschule Fresenius. Retrieved from: http://en.koeln.hs-fresenius.de/homepage-cologne.html [Accessed 2 December 2010]

Ghauri, P. and Grønhaug, K. (2010) *Research Methods in Business Studies*. 4th ed. Harlow: Pearson Education.

Gill, J. and Johnson, P. (2010) *Research Methods for Managers.* 4th ed. London: Sage Publications.

Gladwell, M. (2008) *Outliers: The story of success.* New York: Little, Brown and Company.

Gooderham, P. and Nordhaug, O. (2001) 'Are Cultural Differences in Europe on the Decline?', *European Business Forum,* No. 8, pp.48-53.

Hall, E.T. (1976) *Beyond Culture.* Garden City: Anchor Press/ Doubleday.

Hall, E.T. and Hall, M.R. (1989) *Understanding Cultural Differences: German, French and American.* Yarmouth: Intercultural Press.

Harvey, F. (1997) 'National cultural differences in theory and practice: Evaluating Hofstede's national cultural framework', *Information Technology & People*, Vol. 10, No. 2, pp. 132-146.

Held, D. (2000) *A globalizing world? Culture, economics, politics: An introduction to the social sciences: Understanding social sciences.* New York: Routledge.

Hodgetts, R.M. and Luthans, F. (2003) *International Strategy: Culture, Strategy, and Behavior.* 5th ed. New York: McGraw Hill.

Hoecklin, L. (1995) *Managing Cultural Differences: Strategies for Competitive Advantage.* 2nd ed. Singapore: Addison-Wesley Publishers.

Hofstede, G. (1980) *Culture's Consequences: International Differences in Work-Related Values.* London: Sage Publications.

Hofstede, G. (1983) 'The Cultural Relativity of Organizational Practices and Theories', *Journal of International Business Studies,* Vol. 14, No. 2, pp. 75-89.

Hofstede, G. (1991) *Cultures and Organizations: Software of the mind.* London: McGraw-Hill.

Hofstede, G. (1996) *Cultures and Organizations: Software of the Mind: Intercultural Cooperation and Its Importance for Survival.* New York: McGraw-Hill.

Hofstede, G. (2001) *Cultures Consequences: Comparing Values, Behaviors, Institutions and Organizations Across Nations.* 2nd ed. London: Sage Publications.

Hofstede, G. (2002) 'Dimensions do not exists: A reply to Brendan McSweeney', *Human Relations*, Vol. 55, No. 1, pp. 1-7.

Hofstede, G. (2006) 'What did GLOBE really measure? Researchers' mind versus respondents' minds', *Journal of International Business Studies,* Vol. 37, No. 6, pp. 882-896.

Hofstede, G. (2007) 'Intercultural Co-operation in Organisations', *Employee Relations*, Vol. 1, No. 1, pp. 53-67.

Hofstede, G. (2009a) 'American culture and the 2008 financial crisis', *European Business Review*, Vol. 21, No. 4, pp. 307-312.

Hofstede, G. (2009b) *What are the practical applications for Geert Hofstede's research on cultural differences?* [Online]. Geert Hofstede. Retrieved from: http://www.geert-hofstede.com/ [Accessed 17 December].

Hofstede, G. and Hofstede, G.J. (2004) *Cultures and Organizations: Software of the Mind: Intercultural Cooperation and Its Importance for Survival. 2nd ed.* London: McGraw-Hill.

Hofstede, G. and Hofstede, G.J. (2009) *Dimensions of national culture* [Online]. Geert Hofstede. Retrieved from: http://www.geerthofstede.nl/culture/dimensions-of-national-cultures.aspx [Accessed 8 December 2010].

Hofstede, G. and Hofstede, G.J. (2010) *Dimension Data Matric* [Online]. Geert Hofstede. Retrieved from: http://www.geerthofstede.nl/research--vsm/dimension-data-matrix.aspx [Accessed 8 December 2010].

Hofstede, G., Neuijen, B., Ohayv, D.D. and Sanders, G. (1990) 'Measuring Organizational Cultures: A Qualitative and Quantitative Study across Twenty Cases', *Administrative Science Quarterly*, Vol.35, No. 2, pp. 286-316.

Hofstede, G., Hofstede, G.J. and Pedersen, P.B. (2002) *Exploring Culture: Exercises, Stories and Synthetic Cultures.* London: Nicholas Brealey.

Hofstede, G., van Deusen, C.A., Mueller, C.B., Charles, T.A. and The Business Goals Network (2002) 'What goals do business leaders pursue? A study in fifteen countries', *Journal of International Business Studies,* Vol. 33 No. 4, pp. 785-803.

Hofstede, G., Hofstede, G.J., Minkov, M. and Vinken, H. (2008a) VSM 2008: *Values Survey Module 2008 Manual* [Online]. VSM 08. Retrieved from: http://www.geerthofstede.nl/research--vsm/vsm-08.aspx [Accessed 16 November 2010].

Hofstede, G., Hofstede, G.J., Minkov, M. and Vinken, H. (2008b) *VSM08: VALUES SURVEY MODULE 2008, QUESTIONNAIRE, English language version* [Online]. VSM 08. Retrieved from: http://www.geerthofstede.nl/research--vsm/vsm-08.aspx [Accessed 16 November 2010].

Hofstede, G., Hofstede, G.J. and Minkov, M. (2010) *Cultures and Organizations: Software of the mind: Intercultural Cooperation and its Importance for Survival.* 3rd ed. London: McGraw-Hill.

Hofstede, G. and de Mooij, M. (2010) 'The Hofstede model. Applications to global branding and advertising strategy and research', *International Journal of Advertising*, Vol. 29, No.1, pp. 85-110.

House, R.J., Hanges, P.J., Javidan, M., Dorfman, P.W. and Gupta, V. (2004) *Culture, Leadership, and Organizations. The GLOBE Study of 62 Societies.* London: Sage Publications.

Inglehart, R. (2000) 'World values surveys and European values surveys, 1981–1984, 1990–1993, and 1995–1997 ICPSR Version', *Ann Arbor, MI: Institute for Social Research.*

Jones, M.L. (2007) 'Hofstede - Culturally questionable'. Paper presented at Faculty of Commerce Oxford Business & Economics Conference, University of Wollongong, Oxford, June.

Kluckhohn, C. (1951) *The study of culture.* In Lerner, D. and Lasswell, H.D. (eds) *The policy sciences* (pp.86-101). Stanford, CA: Stanford University Press.

Kluckhohn, C., Strodtbeck, F.L. (1961) *Variations in Value Orientations.* Evanston: Row, Peterson.

Knudsen, L. and Loloma, F. (2007) 'The Human element in Maritime Accidents and disasters - a matter of communication'. Paper presented at The International Maritime Lecturers' Association and the International Maritime English Conference, May, pp. 303-311.

Kogut, B., Singh, H. (1988) 'The Effect of National Culture on the Choice of Entry Mode', *Journal of International Business Studies,* Vol. 19, No. 3, pp. 411-432.

Konopaske, R. and Ivancevich, J.M. (2004) *Global management and organizational behavior.* New York: McGraw Hill.

Kroeber, A.L. and Kluckhohn, C. (1952) *The concept of culture: A critical review of definitions.* Cambridge: Harvard University, Peabody Museum of American Archeology and Ethnology.

Kruger, F., Welman, C. and Mitchell, B. (2005) *Research Methodology.* 3rd ed. Oxford: University Press.

Kuhn, T.S. (1962) *The Structure of Scientific Revolutions.* Chicago: University of Chicago Press.

Kuhn, T.S. (1970) *The Structure of Scientific Revolutions.* 2nd ed. Chicago: University of Chicago Press.

Leidner, D. E. (2010) 'Globalization, culture, and information: Towards global knowledge transparency', *Journal of Strategic Information Systems,* Vol. 19, No. 1, pp. 69-77.

Levitin, T. (1973) 'Values', in J.P. Robinson and P.R. Shaver, Measures of Social Psychological Attitudes, *Survey Research Center,* University of Michigan: Ann Arbor MI, pp. 489–502.

Lewis, R. D. (1996) *When cultures collide: Managing successfully across cultures.* London: Nicholas Brealey Publishing.

Loudon, D.L., Stevens, R.E. and Wrenn, B. (2007) *Marketing Research: Text and Cases.* 2nd ed. Binghampton: Best Business books.

Martin, J. (1992) *Cultures in Organizations: Three perspectives.* Oxford: Oxford University Press.

McBurney, D.H. and White, T.L. (2010) *Research Methods.* 8th ed. Wadsworth: Cengage Learning.

McNeil, P. and Chapman, S. (2005) *Research Methods.* 3rd ed. Abingdon: Routledge.

McSweeney, B. (2002) 'Hofstede's model of national cultural differences and their consequences: a triumph of faith- a failure of analysis', *Human Relations*, Vol. 55, No. 1, pp. 89-118.

Moulettes, A. (2007) *'The absence of women's voices in Hofstede's Cultural Consequences: A postcolonial reading',* Women in Management Review, Vol. 22, No. 6, pp. 443-455.

Mulllins, L.J. (2007) *Management and Organisational Behaviour.* 8th ed. Harlow: Pearson Education.

Myers, M.D. and Tan, F. (2002) 'Beyond models of national culture in information system research', *Journal of Global Information Management*, Vol.10, No.1, pp. 24-32.

Nakata, C. (2009) *Beyond Hofstede: Cultural Frameworks for Global Marketing and Management.* Basingstoke: Palgrave Macmillan.

Nasif, E. G., H. Al-Daeaj, B., Ebrahimi and M. S. Thibodeaux (1991) 'Methodological Problems in Cross-Cultural Research: An Update', *Management International Review*, Vol. 31, No. 1, p. 79.

Neumann, A. (2008) *Die Kulturkonzeption von G. Hofstede: Eine kritische Betrachtung. Saarbrücken*: VDM Verlag Dr. Müller.

Onkvisit, S. and Shaw, J.S. (2004) *International Marketing: Analysis and Strategy.* 2nd ed. Abingdon: Routledge.

Oxford Brookes University (2000) *Ethical standards for research involving human participants. Code of practice* [Online]. Oxford Brookes University. Retrieved from: http://www.brookes.ac.uk/res/policy/ethics_codeofpractice.pdf [Accessed 4 December 2010]

Oxford Brookes University (2010) *Oxford Brookes University Tuition fee* [Online]. Oxford Brookes University. Retrieved from: http://www.brookes.ac.uk/studying/finance/tuition/home [Accessed 2December 2010]

Parhizgar, K. D. (2002) *Multicultural behaviour and global business environments*. New York: The Haworth Press.

Patzer, G. (1996) *Using Secondary data in Market Research: United Stated and World-wide*. Westport: Quorum Books.

Peterson, B. (2004) *Cultural Intelligence: A guide to working with people from other cultures*. London: Nicholas Brealey Publishing.

Peterson, M.F. (2007) 'The Heritage of Cross Cultural Management Research. Implications for the Hofstede Chair in Cultural Diversity', *International Journal of Cross Cultural Management*, Vol. 7, No. 3, pp. 359-377.

Powell, S. (2006) 'Geert Hofstede: challenges of cultural diversity', *Human Resource Management International Digest*, Vol. 14, No. 3, pp. 12-15.

Punch, K.F. (2005) *Introduction to social research: Quantitative and qualitative approaches*. 2nd ed. London: Sage Publications.

Robinson, R. (1983) 'Culture's Consequences', *Work and Occupations*, Vol. 10, No. 1, pp.110-115.

Robson, C. (2002) *Real World Research*. 2nd ed. Oxford: Blackwell Publishing.

Rugman, A. M. (2003) 'Regional strategy and the demise of globalization', *Journal of International Management*, Vol. 9, No. 4, pp. 409-417.

Rugman, A. M. (2005) *The Regional Multinationals: MNEs and "Global" Strategic Sanagement*. Cambridge: Cambridge University Press.

Sagiv, L. and Schwartz, S.H. (2000) 'A New Look at National Culture: Illustrative Applications to Role Stress and Managerial Behavior'. In Ashkanasy, N.M., Wilderom, C.P.M., and Peterson, M.F. *Handbook of Organizational Culture & Climate,* Thousand Oaks: Sage Publications.

Saunders, M., Lewis, P. and Thornhill, A. (2009) *Research methods for business students*. 5th ed. Harlow: Person Education.

Scheuch, E. K. (1996) *Theoretical implications of comparative survey in research: why the wheel of cross-cultural methodology keeps on being reinvented*. In A. Inkeles, and M. Sasaki, *Comparing nations and cultures; readings in a cross disciplinary perspective*. New Jersey: Prentice Hall.

Schein, E.H. (1985) *Organizational Culture and Leadership*. San Francisco: Jossey-Bass.

Schein, E.H. (2010) *Organizational Culture and Leadership*. 4th ed. San Francisco, CA: John Wiley & Sons, Inc.

Schlevogt, K. (2002) *The Art of Chinese Management*. Oxford: Oxford University Press.

Schmidt, M.J. and Hollensen, S. (2006) *Marketing Research: An International Approach*. Harlow: Pearson Education.

Scholte, J. A. (2000) *Globalization: A critical introduction*. London: MacMillan Press.

Schwartz, S.H. (1992) 'Universals in the Content and Structure of Values: Theoretical Advances and Empirical Tests in 20 Countries'. In Zanna, M.P. *Advances in Experimental Social Psychology*, Vol. 25, No. 1, pp. 1-65.

Schwartz, S. H. (1999) 'A Theory of Cultural Values and Some Implications for Work', *Applied Psychology*, Vol. 48, No. 1, pp. 23-47.

Shane S. A. (1993) 'Cultural influences on national rates of innovation', *Journal of Business Venturing,* Vol. 8, No. 1, pp. 59-73.

Søndergaard, M. (1994) 'Hofstede's consequences: A study of reviews, citations and replications', *Organization Studies,* Vol.15, No. 3, pp. 447- 449.

Søndergaard, M. (2010) *Dr. Geert Hofstede™ Cultural Dimensions* [Online]. Geert Hofstede. Retrieved from http://geert-hofstede.international-business-center.com/Sondergaard.shtml [Accessed 21 April 2010].

Stevens, J. M. and Bird, A. (2004) 'On the myth of believing that globalization is a myth: or the effects of misdirected response on obsolescing an emergent substantive discourse', *Journal of International Management,* Vol. 10, No. 5, pp. 501-510.

Swetman, D. and Swetman, R. (2009) *Writing your dissertation. The bestselling guide to planning, preparing and presenting first-class work.* 3rd ed. Oxford: How to books.

Swierczek, F.W. (1994) 'The Praxis of Cross-cultural Management', *Cross Cultural Management: An International Journal,* Vol. 1, No. 1, pp. 14-19.

Taras, V. and Steel, P. (2009) 'Beyond Hofstede: Challenging the ten commandments of cross-cultural Research'. In Nakata, C. (2009) *Beyond Hofstede: Cultural Frameworks for Global Marketing and Management.* Basingstoke: Palgrave Macmillan

Tayeb, M.H. (1996) 'Hofstede'. In Warner, M., International Encyclopaedia of Business and Management. London: Thomson Press, Vol. 2, No.1, pp.1771-1776.

Thomas, D.C. and Inkson, K. (2003) *Cultural Intelligence. People Skills for global business.* San Francisco: Berrett-Koehler Publishers.

Triandis, H.C. (1994) *Culture and Social Behaviour.* London: McGraw-Hill.

Triandis, H.C. (2004) 'The many dimensions of Culture', *Academy of Management,* Vol. 35, No. 2, pp.145-152.

Trompenaars, F. and Hampden-Turner, C. (1997) *Riding the waves of culture: Understanding cultural diversity in global business.* 2nd ed. London: Nicholas Brealey Publishing.

Von der Gracht, H.A. (2008) *The Future of Logistics. Scenarios for 2025.* Wiesbaden: Gabler Edition Wissenschaft.

Warner, M. and Joynt, P. (2002) *Managing Across Cultures. Issues and Perspectives.* 2nd ed. London: Thomson Learning.

Wederspahn, G.M. (2000) *Intercultural Services. A Worldwide Buyer's Guide and Sourcebook.* Houston, Texas: Gulf Publishing.

Wildavsky, A. (1998) 'Frames of reference come from cultures: a predicative theory'. In Freilichs, M. *'The relevance of culture'* (pp.58-74). New York: Bergin And Gravey.

Wu, M. (2006) 'Hofstede's Cultural Dimensions 30 Years Later: A study of Taiwan and the United States', *Intercultural Communication Studies*, Vol. 15, No.1, pp. 33-42.

APPENDICES

APPENDIX A:

CULTURAL DIMENSION SCORES

COUNTRY	PDI	IDV	MAS	UA	LTO	IVR
Africa East*	64	27	41	52	32	40
Afria West**	77	20	46	54	9	78
Arab countries***	80	38	53	68	23	34
Argentina	49	46	56	86	20	62
Australia	36	90	61	51	21	71
Austria	11	55	79	70	60	63
Bangladesh	80	20	55	60	47	20
Belgium	65	75	54	94	82	57
Brazil	69	38	49	76	44	59
Bulgaria	70	30	40	85	69	16
Canada	39	80	52	48	36	68
Chile	63	23	28	86	31	68
China	80	20	66	30	87	24
Colombia	67	13	64	80	13	83
Croatia	73	33	40	80	58	33
Czech Rep	57	58	57	74	70	29
Denmark	18	74	16	23	35	70
El Salvador	66	19	40	94	20	89
Estonia	40	60	30	60	82	16
Finland	33	63	26	59	38	57
France	68	71	43	86	63	48
Germany	**35**	**67**	**66**	**65**	**83**	**40**
Great Britain	**35**	**89**	**66**	**35**	**51**	**69**
Greece	60	35	57	112	45	50
Hong Kong	68	25	57	29	61	17
Hungary	46	80	88	82	58	31
India	77	48	56	40	51	26
Indonesia	78	14	46	48	62	38
Iran	58	41	43	59	14	40
Ireland	28	70	68	35	24	65
Italy	50	76	70	75	61	30
Japan	54	46	95	92	88	42
Korea South	60	18	39	85	100	29
Latvia	44	70	9	63	69	13
Lithuania	42	60	19	65	82	16
Luxembourg	40	60	50	70	64	56
Malaysia	104	26	50	36	41	57
Malta	56	59	47	96	47	66
Mexico	81	30	69	82	24	97
Morocco	70	46	53	68	14	25
Netherlands	38	80	14	53	67	68
New Zealand	22	79	58	49	33	75
Norway	31	69	8	50	35	55
Pakistan	55	14	50	70	50	0
Peru	64	16	42	87	25	46
Philippines	94	32	64	44	27	42

Poland	68	60	64	93	38	29
Portugal	63	27	31	104	28	33
Romania	90	30	42	90	52	20
Russia	93	39	36	95	81	20
Serbia	86	25	43	92	52	28
Singapore	74	20	48	8	72	46
Slovak Rep	104	52	110	51	77	28
Slovenia	71	27	19	88	49	48
Spain	57	51	42	86	48	44
Sweden	31	71	5	29	53	78
Switzerland	34	68	70	58	74	66
Taiwan	58	17	45	69	93	49
Thailand	64	20	34	64	32	45
Turkey	66	37	45	85	46	49
U.S.A.	40	91	62	46	26	68
Uruguay	61	36	38	100	26	53
Venezuela	81	12	73	76	16	100
Vietnam	70	20	40	30	57	35

(Source: Hofstede and Hofstede, 2010)

*East Africa = Ethiopia, Kenya, Tanzania, Zambia
**West Africa = Ghana, Nigeria, Sierra Leone
***Arab World = Egypt, Iraq, Kuwait, Lebanon, Libya, Saudi Arabia, United Arab Emirates

APPENDIX B:

INFORMATION SHEET FOR THE QUESTIONNAIRE

Title: **Survey about cultural dimension at Oxford Brookes University**

Oxford, 25th November, 2010

Dear Students,

You are being invited to take part in a postgraduate research project that forms part of my assessment for my degree. Before you decide whether or not to take part, it is important for you to understand why the research is being done and what it will involve. Please take time to read the following information carefully.

The purpose if my study is to identify cultural dimension in the United Kingdom and specifically at the Oxford Brookes University. This study involves around 170 students at the University.

It is up to you to decide whether or not to take part. If you do decide to take part you will be given this information sheet to keep. If you decide to take part you are still free to withdraw at any time and without giving a reason.

The questionnaire will take approximately 5-10 minutes and you are asked to give your own opinion about university- and work-related questions.

The answers will kept strictly confidential and privacy and anonymity will be ensured in the collection, storage and publication of research material.

I am conducting the research as a student at the Oxford Brookes University and this research is part of my assessment for my Master of Science degree in Business Management.

If you would like to take part in the survey and help me to add value to my master thesis then I would be grateful if you could answer the questions on the following pages.

If you have any further questions or concerns, please do not hesitate to contact me.

Thank you very much for taking the time to read the information sheet.

Kristin Piepenburg

APPENDIX C:

QUESTIONNAIRE ENGLISH

1 How often do you feel nervous or tense at work or at university?

Please tick ☐ the box that matches your view most closely

I always feel this way	Usually	Sometimes	Seldom	I never feel this way	Do not know
☐	☐	☐	☐	☐	☐

2 How long do you think you will stay in the first company you are working for?

Please tick ☐ the box that matches your view most closely

☐ Two years at most

☐ From two to five years

☐ More than five years (but I will probably leave before I retire)

☐ Until I retire

☐ Do not know

3 Do you agree or disagree with the following statement:

"Company rules should not be broken- even when the employee thinks it is in the company's best interest"

Please tick ☐ the box that matches your view most closely

strongly agree	agree	undecided	disagree	strongly disagree	Do not know
☐	☐	☐	☐	☐	☐

| 4 | Which statement do you tend to agree more:

Please tick ☐ the box that matches your view most closely

- ☐ I feel more comfortable with open-ended learning situations and am concerned with good discussions

- ☐ I feel more comfortable in structured learning situations and concerned with the right answers

- ☐ Do not know

| 5 | Which statement do you tend to agree more:

Please tick ☐ the box that matches your view most closely

- ☐ Teacher's may say, "I don't know"
- ☐ Teachers are supposed to have all the answers

- ☐ Do not know

| 6 | Which statement do you tend to agree more:

Please tick ☐ the box that matches your view most closely

- ☐ I prefer to have a strict timetable and detailed assignment tasks
- ☐ I prefer to have no timetable and broad assignment tasks
- ☐ Do not know

| 7 | Which statement do you tend to agree more:

Please tick ☐ the box that matches your view most closely

- ☐ Teachers should involve parents in their children's learning process
- ☐ Teachers should inform parents about their children's learning process

- ☐ Do not know

| 8 | Which statement do you tend to agree more: |

Please tick ☐ the box that matches your view most closely

[I feel more comfortable in a structured and rule-dominated environment

[I feel more comfortable in a unstructured environment and there should be no more rules than strictly necessary

[Do not know

| 9 | Try to think of those factors that would be important to you in an ideal job; disregard the extent to which they are contained in your present job. |

From the list of factors below, please tick ☐ the three most important ones for you and rank them 1, 2, 3:

	1.	2.	3.
- Good pay	☐	☐	☐
- An opportunity to use initiative	☐	☐	☐
- A job respected by people in general	☐	☐	☐
- Generous holidays	☐	☐	☐
- Good job security	☐	☐	☐
- Not too much pressure	☐	☐	☐
- Good working hours	☐	☐	☐
- A job which you feel you can achieve something	☐	☐	☐

10 Try to think of those factors that would be important to you in an ideal job; disregard the extent to which they are contained in your present job. How important is it to you:

Please tick ☐ the box that matches your view most closely

	Of utmost importance to me	Very important	Of moderate importance	Of little important	Of very little or no importance	Do not know
- **Earnings**: have an opportunity for high earnings	☐	☐	☐	☐	☐	☐
- **Recognition**: get the recognition you deserve when you do a good job	☐	☐	☐	☐	☐	☐
- **Advancement**: have an opportunity for advancement to higher-level jobs	☐	☐	☐	☐	☐	☐
- **Challenge**: have challenging work to do- work from which you can get a personal sense of accomplishment	☐	☐	☐	☐	☐	☐
- **Working relationship with manager**: Have a good working relationship with your direct superiors	☐	☐	☐	☐	☐	☐
- **Cooperation**: work with people who cooperate well with one another	☐	☐	☐	☐	☐	☐
- **Living area**: live in an area desirable to you and your family	☐	☐	☐	☐	☐	☐
- **Employment security**: have the security that you will be able to work for your company as long as you want to	☐	☐	☐	☐	☐	☐

11 How old are you?

---

12 Are you:

☐ Male

☐ Female

---

13 Where are you from:

☐ Germany

☐ United Kingdom

☐ Others: _____

---

14 In which country did you grow up?
if more than one please write below in detail where and how long.

Main country where i grew up _____

Other countries where i was growing up _____

---

15 What are your parents' nationalities?

Mother _____

Father _____

16 What is your current occupation?

(Multiple answers are possible)

- ☐ Student (full time)
- ☐ Student (part time)
- ☐ Working full time
- ☐ Working part time
- ☐ Others: _____

17 What level of degree are you currently studying for?

(e.g. Bachelor of Arts in Business Management)

_____

18 Do you have any work experience?

- ☐ Internship
- ☐ Part-time job
- ☐ Holiday job
- ☐ Voluntary work
- ☐ full-time job
- ☐ Others: _____

Thank you very much for your participation.

APPENDIX D:

QUESTIONNAIRE GERMAN

1 Wie häufig bist Du bei der Arbeit oder in der Universität nervös oder angespannt?

Bitte mache ein Häkchen ☐ in das Feld, welches deiner Meinung am ehesten entspricht

Immer	Oft	Manchmal	Selten	Nie	Ich weiß es nicht
☐	☐	☐	☐	☐	☐

2 Wie lange wirst Du deiner Einschätzung nach für das erste Unternehmen, bei dem du angestellt wirst arbeiten?

Bitte mache ein Häkchen ☐ in das Feld, welches deiner Meinung am ehesten entspricht

- ☐ Höchstens zwei Jahre
- ☐ Zwei bis fünf Jahre
- ☐ Mehr als fünf Jahre (aber ich werde wahrscheinlich vor meiner Pensionierung kündigen)
- ☐ Bis zu meiner Pensionierung
- ☐ Ich weiß es nicht

3 Inwiefern stimmst Du der folgenden Aussage zu:

"Gegen im Unternehmen bestehende Regeln darf nicht verstoßen werden – auch wenn der Mitarbeiter der Meinung ist, es geschehe zum Besten der Firma"

Bitte mache ein Häkchen ☐ in das Feld, welches deiner Meinung am ehesten entspricht

Stimme vollstens zu	Stimme zu	Unentschlossen	Stimme nicht zu	Stimme überhaupt nicht zu	Ich weiß es nicht
☐	☐	☐	☐	☐	☐

4 Welcher Aussage würdest Du eher zustimmen?

Bitte mache ein Häkchen ☐ in das Feld, welches deiner Meinung am ehesten entspricht

☐ Ich fühle mich wohler in Lernsituationen mit offenen Ausgängen und interessiere mich für angeregte Diskussionen

☐ Ich fühle mich wohler in strukturierten Lernsituationen und interessiere mich für korrekte Antworten

☐ Ich weiß es nicht

5 Welcher Aussage würdest Du eher zustimmen?

Bitte mache ein Häkchen ☐ in das Feld, welches deiner Meinung am ehesten entspricht

☐ Lehrer dürfen sagen: "Ich weiß es nicht"

☐ Lehrer sollen eine Antwort auf jede Frage haben

☐ Ich weiß es nicht

6 Welcher Aussage würdest Du eher zustimmen:

Bitte mache ein Häkchen ☐ in das Feld, welches deiner Meinung am ehesten entspricht

☐ Ich bevorzuge einen strikten Stundenplan und detaillierte Aufgabenstellungen

☐ Ich bevorzuge keinen Stundenplan und weit gefasste Aufgabenstellungen

☐ Ich weiß es nicht

7 Welcher Aussage würdest Du eher zustimmen?

Bitte mache ein Häkchen ☐ in das Feld, welches deiner Meinung am ehesten entspricht

☐ Lehrer sollten Eltern in den Lernprozess ihrer Kinder einbeziehen

☐ Lehrer sollten Eltern über den Lernprozess ihrer Kinder informieren

☐ Ich weiß es nicht

8 Welcher Aussage würdest Du eher zustimmen?

Bitte mache ein Häkchen ☐ in das Feld, welches deiner Meinung am ehesten entspricht

[ ] Ich fühle mich wohler in einer strukturierten und Regelorientierten Umwelt

[ ] Ich fühle mich wohler in einer unstrukturierten Umwelt und es sollten nur so viele Regeln geben wie unbedingt nötig

[ ] Ich weiß es nicht

9 Denke an die Faktoren, die dir im idealen Job wichtig wären; unabhängig davon in welchem Ausmaß diese vorhanden sind in deinem jetzigen Job.

Bitte wähle aus den folgenden Faktoren drei aus, die Dir am wichtigsten sind und bringe sie in die Reihenfolge 1, 2, 3:

	1.	2.	3.
- Gute Bezahlung	☐	☐	☐
- Möglichkeit Initiative zu zeigen	☐	☐	☐
- Ein Job, der angesehen ist	☐	☐	☐
- Großzügige Urlaubstage	☐	☐	☐
- Gute Jobsicherheit	☐	☐	☐
- Nicht zu viel Druck	☐	☐	☐
- Gute Arbeitszeiten	☐	☐	☐
- Ein Job in dem Du was erreichen kannst	☐	☐	☐

10 Denke an die Faktoren, die Dir im idealen Job wichtig wären und bewerte Ihre Wichtigkeit

Bitte mache ein Häkchen ☐ in das Feld, welches deiner Meinung am ehesten entspricht

	Äußerst wichtig	Sehr wichtig	Wichtig	Geringe Wichtigkeit	Sehr geringe oder keine Wichtigkeit	Ich weiß es nicht
- **Einkommen**: die Möglichkeit, viel zu verdienen	☐	☐	☐	☐	☐	☐
- **Anerkennung**: die Anerkennung zu bekommen, die man verdient, wenn man gute Arbeit geleistet hat	☐	☐	☐	☐	☐	☐
- **Beförderung**: die Möglichkeit zu haben, in höhere Positionen aufzusteigen	☐	☐	☐	☐	☐	☐
- **Herausforderung**: bei der Arbeit gefordert zu werden – eine Arbeit zu haben, die einen zufrieden stellt.	☐	☐	☐	☐	☐	☐
- **Arbeitsverhältnis mit dem Chef**: ein gutes Arbeitsverhältnis mit dem direkten Vorgesetzten zu haben	☐	☐	☐	☐	☐	☐
- **Zusammenarbeit**: mit Kollegen gut zusammenarbeiten	☐	☐	☐	☐	☐	☐
- **Wohngegend**: in einer für sich selbst und die Familie angenehmen und freundlichen Umgebung zu leben	☐	☐	☐	☐	☐	☐
- **Sicherheit des Arbeitsplatzes**: das sichere Gefühl zu haben, solange beim Arbeitgeber bleiben zu können, wie man will.	☐	☐	☐	☐	☐	☐

11 Wie alt bist Du?

---

12 Bist Du

☐ Männlich

☐ Weiblich

13 Woher kommst Du?

☐ Deutschland

☐ Großbritannien

☐ Sonstiges:

14 In welchem Land bist du aufgewachsen?
Falls in mehr als einem, bitte erläutere genau wo und wie lange

Land, in dem ich
aufgewachsen bin

Weitere Länder, in
denen ich
aufgewachsen bin

15 Welcher Nationalität gehören Deine Eltern an?

Falls mehr als eine, bitte konkretisiere

Mutter
Vater

| 16 | Was ist Deine derzeitige Beschäftigung?

(Mehrere Antworten möglich)

- ☐ Student (Vollzeitig)
- ☐ Student (Teilzeitig)
- ☐ Vollzeitig berufstätig
- ☐ Teilzeitig berufstätig
- ☐ Sonstiges: _____

| 17 | Für welchen akademischen Abschluss studierest du derzeitig?

(z.B.: *Bachelor of Arts in Business Management*)

_____

| 18 | Hast Du irgendeine Art von Arbeitserfahrung?

- ☐ Praktikum
- ☐ Teilzeitjob
- ☐ Ferienjob
- ☐ freiwillige Arbeit
- ☐ Vollzeitjob
- ☐ Sonstiges: _____

Vielen herzlichen Dank für deine Teilnahme.

APPENDIX E:

THE UNIVERSITY CODE OF 'ETHICAL STANDARDS FOR RESEARCH INVOLVING HUMAN PARTICIPANTS'

Ethical standards for research involving human participants
Code of practice

1. Introduction

1.1 The integrity of any research depends not only on its scientific rigour, but also on its ethical adequacy. Ethical issues are many and varied, and may be quite complex. Research involving human participants is undertaken by many different disciplines and conducted in a broad range of settings and institutions. While some issues are specific to professional groups, all research should be guided by a set of fundamental ethical principles to ensure the protection of human participants.

1.2 Underpinning the standards are the ethical imperatives of DO NO HARM (nonmaleficience) and DO GOOD (beneficience). Consideration of risks versus benefits need to be weighed up by researchers. In medical research physically invasive procedures are easily defined, but what constitutes risk in social research is sometimes less clear cut. Questionnaires, observation and interviews can all be potentially intrusive and provoke anxiety in participants, or worse, involve psychological risk. It is important to think through carefully the likely impact on participants of any data collection methods. Certain groups are particularly vulnerable and may succumb to pressure, for example students, children or people with learning disability. Some participants are unable to give informed consent and are therefore less able to protect themselves, for example people with dementia. Research activities may be so unintrusive that individual consent is not warranted, such as in the case of some community-based studies.

1.3 The following standards have been developed to guide staff and students undertaking research involving human participants. They are intended to cover general principles, but they may not address all situations and the researcher should seek further advice from their School's Research Ethics Officer, the University Research Ethics Committee and their profession's code of practice for research ethics as appropriate.

2. No research should cause harm, and preferably it should benefit participants

2.1 A judgement needs to be made as to whether a particular intervention is likely to affect the well-being of participants and any potential risks to participants which might arise in the course of the research should be identified.

2.2 Procedures must be justified, explaining why alternative approaches involving less risk cannot be used.

2.3 The potential benefits of the research to participants, the scientific community and/or society must be clearly stated.

2.4 Any cultural, religious, gender or other differences in a research population should be sensitively and appropriately handled by researchers at all stages.

Ethical standards for research involving human participants 1 of 6

3. Potential participants normally have the right to receive clearly communicated information from the researcher in advance

3.1 Most research procedures should be explained on an information sheet written in simple language that is easily comprehensible by the potential research participant.

3.2 The information sheet should set out: the purpose of the investigation; the procedures; the risks (including psychological distress); the benefits, or absence of them, to the individual or to others in the future or to society; a statement that individuals may decline to participate and also will be free to withdraw at any time without giving a reason; and an invitation to ask questions.

3.3 The information sheet should also provide contact details of the School's Research Ethics Officer so that participants may report any procedures that seem to violate their welfare.

3.4 Participants should be given plenty of time to study the information sheet, and consult relevant parties.

3.5 The information sheet and the consent form (see Appendix) should form part of the application for ethics approval.

4. Participants should be free from coercion of any kind and should not be pressured to participate in a study

4.1 Promises of compensation and care for damage, injury or loss of income should not be considered inducements.

4.2 Inducements, such as special services or financial payments (other than reimbursement for travel expenses or in some cases time), and the creation of inappropriate motivation should usually be avoided.

4.3 Risks involved in participation should be acceptable to participants, even in the absence of inducement.

4.4 Reimbursement of participants' expenses, for example for journeys, is not payment in the sense of reward, and can be provided.

4.5 Participants must be free to withdraw from the study at any time.

5. Participants in a research study have the right to give their informed consent before participating

5.1 Participants should understand the purpose and nature of the study, what participation in the study requires, and what benefits are intended to result from the study (see section 6 for special guidance on vulnerable participants and section 7 for exceptional circumstances).

5.2 Voluntary informed consent, in writing, should usually be obtained from any participant who is able to give such consent (see Appendix).

5.3 It is the researcher's responsibility to seek ongoing consent during the course of a study.

5.4 Consent may be implied by the completion and return of many social survey questionnaires, removing the need for written consent.

5.5 Individual consent may be unnecessary for some research activities, such as community research, which may be quite unintrusive, for example studies involving observation of public behaviour.

6. Where third parties are affected by the research, informal consent should be obtained

6.1 When third parties, for example spouses, teachers or health care professionals, are directly involved in the care, education or treatment of the potential participants, consent should also be obtained from them.

6.2 Informal consent should involve sharing of information about the project.

6.3 If the proposed research is likely to interfere with the treatment or care being provided by a third party, it is necessary that they be fully informed and sign a consent to participate.

6.4 In certain situations, the affiliation of participants to particular organisations or special groups such as educational institutions, business organisations, or hospitals, may necessitate the granting of permission to conduct the research project and any relevant policies or guidelines should be followed.

7. The consent of vulnerable participants or their representatives' assent should be actively sought by researchers

7.1 If the involvement of children in a research study is justified, then parents or other legal guardians have the right to be informed and to give their assent for inclusion of the child in the study.

7.2 In the case of educational research, any special school policies or procedures should be followed.

7.3 To the extent that it is feasible, which will vary with age, the willing consent of participants who are children should also be sought. Generally, children over age 16 may be assumed to be capable of giving informed consent, but this will vary depending on the nature of research and special guidance may need to be sought.

7.4 In cases where people are unable to comprehend the implications of research, for example people with dementia, assent to participate may have to come from a representative, such as a legal guardian or immediate relative.

7.5 Witnessed consent is required for vulnerable participants who have intellectual or cultural difficulties in speech or understanding, but who are deemed capable of giving consent.

7.6 The quality of the consent of participants who are in a potentially dependent relationship with the researcher (e.g. students, employees and patients) requires careful consideration, as willingness to volunteer may be unduly influenced by the expectation of advantageous benefits.

8. Honesty should be central to the relationship between researcher, participant and institutional representatives

8.1 The deception of participants should be avoided.

8.2 The use of one-way mirrors for observation in any investigation must be clearly justified.

Ethical standards for research involving human participants 3 of 6

8.3 If deception is necessary, the reasons should be explained to participants after the study.

9. Participants' confidentiality and anonymity should be maintained

9.1 Researchers should take precautions to protect confidentiality of participants and data.

9.2 The identity of the participant, or any information which may identify the participant, may not be revealed without the participant's adequate prior consent in writing.

9.3 Researchers and other collaborators should deal with all data obtained through their project in such a manner as not to compromise the personal dignity of the participant or to infringe upon the participant's right to privacy.

9.4 All information obtained in the course of a research project should be considered privileged information and should under no circumstances be publicly disclosed in a fashion that would identify any individual or organisation (except if subpoenaed by a court).

9.5 When personal identifiers are used in a study, researchers should explain why this is necessary and how confidentiality would be protected.

9.6 Procedures for protecting the confidentiality of participants should be followed and include:
- securing individual confidentiality statements from all research personnel;
- coding data with numbers instead of names to protect the identity of participants;
- using codes for identification of participants when transcribing audiotapes, and destroying the tapes on completion of transcription;
- storing data with any identifying information in a locked file to which only one or two persons have access;
- using pseudonyms for participants, agencies and geographical settings in the publishing of reports;
- disposing of information that can reveal the identity of participants or places carefully (e.g. burning or shredding rather than disposal in wastebaskets).

10. The collection and storage of research data by researchers must comply with the Data Protection Act 1998

10.1 Researchers should follow the University's Data Protection Policy and Guidelines.

10.2 Researchers should be aware of the risks to anonymity, privacy and confidentiality posed by all kinds of personal information storage and processing, including computer and paper files, e-mail records, audio and videotapes, or any other information which directly identifies an individual.

10.3 Participants must be informed of the kinds of personal information which will be collected, what will be done with it, and to whom it will be disclosed. 'Consent to process' may need to be obtained where information collected from individuals is to be used later for research purposes.

10.4 Measures to prevent accidental breaches of confidentiality should be taken (see section 9), and in cases where confidentiality is threatened, relevant records should be destroyed.

10.5 Provisions for data security at the end of a project must be made. Where the researcher leaves the University, this responsibility should usually rest with the relevant School.

11. Researchers have a duty to disseminate their research findings to all appropriate parties

11.1 Participants and relevant stakeholders should be offered access to a summary of the research findings.

11.2 Reports to the public should be clear and understandable, and accurately reflect the significance of the study.

HB/JC
25.3.00

(Oxford Brookes University, 2000)

APPENDIX F:
DATA EXCEL SHEET

128

130

131

132

133

APPENDIX G:
CHARTS EXCEL SHEET

134

Q.24

4. Which statement do you agree with

	low UA		high UA		
	1	5	1	5	
	36	61	36	61	
	42	54	42	54	
	open ended lea	structured learn			Do not Know

Chartbase
36	61	36	61	9
42	54	42	54	8
36	305	36	305	-
42	270	42	270	-
34%	58%	34%	58%	8%
40%	52%	40%	52%	8%

Avg 3,5 high UA
Avg 3,3 high UA

Question 4: Which statement do you agree with?
- open ended learning: 40% / 34%
- structured learning: 58% / 52%
- Do not Know: 8% / 8%

5. Which statement do you agree with

	low UA		high UA		
	1	5	1	5	
	75	29	75	29	
	51	48	51	48	
	may say "do no	all the answers			Do not Know

Chartbase
75	29	75	29	2
51	48	51	48	5
75	145	75	145	-
51	240	51	240	-
71%	27%	71%	27%	2%
49%	46%	49%	46%	5%

Avg 2,1 low UA
Avg 2,9 low UA

Question 5: Which statement do you agree with?
- may say "do not know": 71% / 49%
- all the answers: 27% / 46%
- Do not Know: 2% / 5%

6. Which statement do you agree with

	low UA		high UA		
	1	5	1	5	
	83	14	83	14	
	80	22	80	22	
	strict timetable	no timetable			Do not Know

Chartbase
83	14	83	14	9
80	22	80	22	2
83	70	83	70	-
80	110	80	110	-
78%	13%	78%	13%	8%
77%	21%	77%	21%	2%

Avg 1,6 high UA
Avg 1,9 high UA

Question 6: Which statement do you agree with?
- strict timetable: 78% / 77%
- no timetable: 13% / 21%
- Do not Know: 8% / 2%

7. Which statement do you agree with

	low UA		high UA		
	1	5	1	5	
	32	61	32	61	
	34	59	34	59	
	involve paren	inform parent			Do not Know

Chartbase
32	61	32	61	11
34	59	34	59	11
32	305	32	305	-
34	295	34	295	-
31%	59%	31%	59%	11%
33%	57%	33%	57%	11%

Avg 3,6 high UA
Avg 3,5 high UA

Question 7: Which statement do you agree with?
- involve parents: 31% / 33%
- inform parents: 59% / 57%
- Do not Know: 11% / 11%

8. Which statement do you agree with

	low UA		high UA		
	1	5	1	5	
	70	30	70	30	
	44	56	44	56	
	structured en	unstructured e			Do not Know

Chartbase
70	30	70	30	6
44	56	44	56	4
70	150	70	150	-
44	280	44	280	-
66%	28%	66%	28%	6%
42%	54%	42%	54%	4%

Avg 2,2 high UA
Avg 3,2 low UA

Question 8: Which statement do you agree with?
- structured environment: 66% / 42%
- unstructured environment: 28% / 54%
- Do not Know: 6% / 4%

135

9. Rank the factors for your ideal job

	mas	mas	fem	fem	fem	fem	mas
	-	64	41	19	105	-	99
	134	79	78	36	69	46	143
	137					14	
						17	57

good pay opportuni respected generous job securi not too m good worl achievem

Chartbase

16%	1%	2%	1%	1%	0%	1%	9%
8%	4%	2%	1%	8%	0%	3%	6%
4%	4%	6%	2%	6%	1%	5%	10%
75	27	28	10	42	3	23	68
19%	1%	0%	0%	2%	2%	0%	8%
8%	7%	4%	3%	3%	1%	2%	6%
3%	4%	6%	2%	5%	1%	5%	9%
93	36	31	16	29	10	22	71

Avg n.a.
Avg n.a.

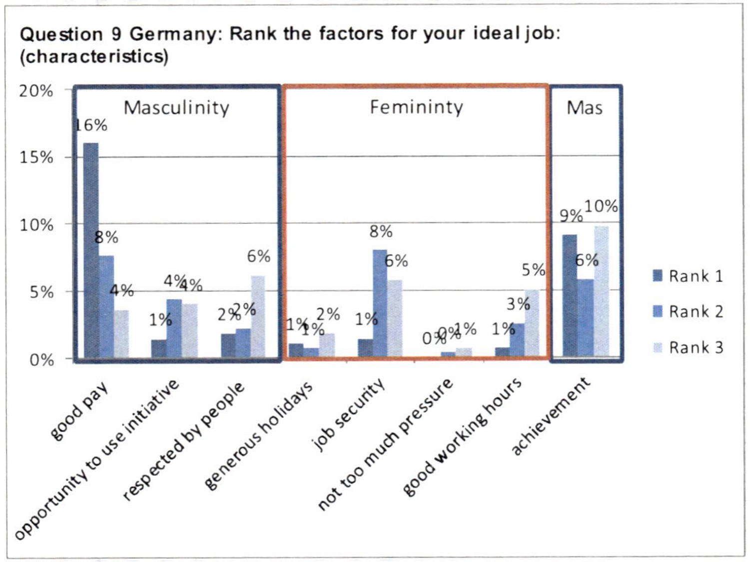

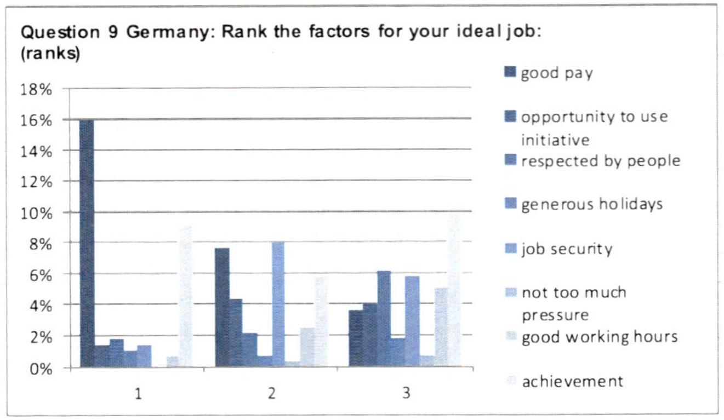

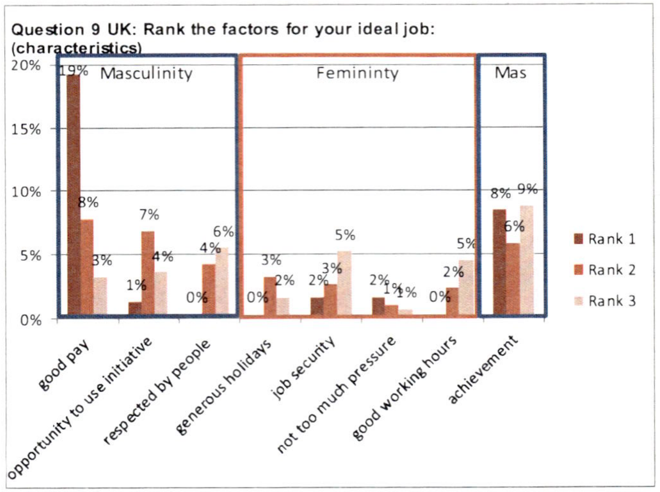

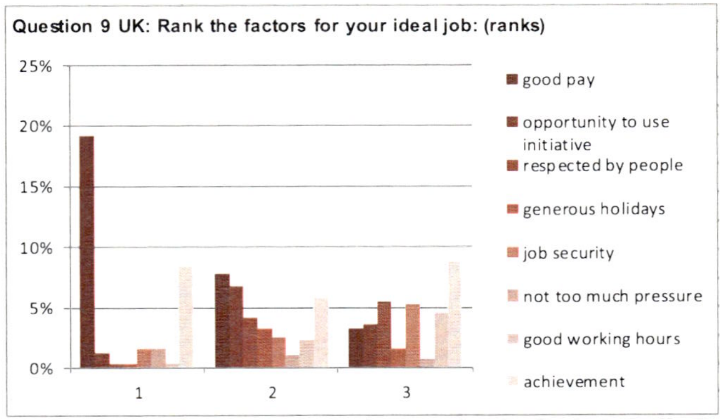

Question 9 Germany: Rank the factors for your ideal job: (ranks)

Question 9 Germany: Rank the factors for your ideal job: (characteristics)

Question 9 UK: Rank the factors for your ideal job: (characteristics)

Question 9 UK: Rank the factors for your ideal job: (ranks)

137

138